"We all leave a legacy. The decisions and actions that legacy and how we are remembered when we depart this earth. In shed book *Recalibrate Your Life*, Kenneth Boa and Jenny Abel provide a comprehensive and robust treatment of this topic. They provide ways to think about your legacy and also tools to help you make it a reality. Start today. Eternity is right around the corner for all of us."

Russ Crosson, chief mission officer of Ronald Blue Trust

"Grounded firmly in Scripture, Ken and Jenny present a compelling case for regular recalibration of our lives and provide practical tools and provocative questions to keep us focused on the grace of God, allowing God to create God's legacy with our lives. This is not only a retirement or end-of-life study guide. It is for all of life: a compass to keep our path true. This book makes you think about life, today and tomorrow."

Walter C. Wright Jr., executive director of the Max De Pree Center for Leadership and author of *Relational Leadership*

"As we are told in Scripture, the Lord our God does not change. However, our lives are subject to change in ways that are both expected and unexpected. We make our plans, but the Lord directs our steps. For those who are searching for solid ground on which to plant their feet, especially during times of movement and transition, *Recalibrate Your Life* is a helpful, thoroughly scriptural field guide."

Scott Sauls, senior pastor of Christ Presbyterian Church and author of *Beautiful People Don't Just Happen*

"Callings are seasonal, not static. If you sense God leading you into a new season, don't embark on the journey without *Recalibrate Your Life*."

Jordan Raynor, author of *Called to Create* and *Redeeming Your Time*

"We would have been lost without it, wandering about and arriving nowhere in particular. *It* was the maps app that guided my family through our first international vacation. And *it* always began by identifying our current location and then offering us proven routes to our desired destinations. *Recalibrate Your Life* is like a maps app for a meaningful life. Chapter after chapter, Boa and Abel help readers assess their current location and move toward their desired destination through tools that are intelligent, practical, and doable. The exercises (which are refreshingly absent of fluff) would be of benefit to all who breathe. But for those in transition, in confusion, or simply in indecision, this book could be the God-magnetized compass you need to take your next step with intention and infuse your next season with meaning."

Alicia Britt Chole, author of *Anonymous: Jesus' Hidden Years . . . and Yours* and *Forty Days of Decrease*

"Ken Boa and Jenny Abel's book is both a scholarly and a personal exhortation to the fact that we as Christians have only one life to live and one chance to live it with the eternal perspective and purpose that will matter at the end. Replete with tools and supporting glimpses into the lives of the authors and others who seek to live with eternally significant intentionality, it isn't, and is not intended to be, a quick fix but a real plan for living as a fruitful disciple."

Buck Jacobs, founder of the C12 Group and author of *A Christian Road Less Traveled*

"Your life is a God-given pilgrimage. Are you walking it with meaning and purpose? Are you investing it wisely in the people God brings your way? Fellow pilgrims Ken Boa and Jenny Abel employ Scripture and experience-based wisdom to enable you to answer yes to these questions. And they offer practical tools to help you recalibrate when you choose a new road or take an unexpected path. No matter how far you've traveled along the trail of life, you'll benefit from this insightful and helpful guidebook. If you want to live well to the glory of God, this book is for you."

James E. Taylor, coauthor of *Soul Pilgrimage: Knowing God in Everyday Life*

"Ken Boa and Jenny Abel offer several tools throughout this book that inspire a paradigm shift in the way we think about our work and calling. From offering practical thoughts on retirement to stewarding our time, talent, treasure, truth, and relationships, Boa and Abel ground everything in the unfailing, everlasting truth of Scripture. There is great wisdom in this book for anyone."

D. Michael Lindsay, president of Taylor University and author of *Hinge Moments: Making the Most of Life's Transitions*

"Ken Boa and Jenny Abel have done it again. At a time when the world has changed as never before, we have a unique opportunity to recalibrate our life, priorities, focus, and purpose; this book provides the wisdom and the way to do just that. I highly recommend it."

Chip Ingram, author of *True Spirituality* and founder and CEO of Living on the Edge

"I, like so many others, find books about life purpose irresistible. Purpose plus me is a compelling combination. Ken Boa and Jenny Abel's book, *Recalibrate Your Life*, sets a new standard for the genre. Every chapter contains a comprehensive overview of God's perspective on the subject, and this—coupled with interesting stories, creative metaphors, and the wisdom of sages across time—brings the content alive in a manner that compels deep reflection on the part of readers of any age."

Pat MacMillan, founder of Triaxia Partners and author of *The Performance Factor*

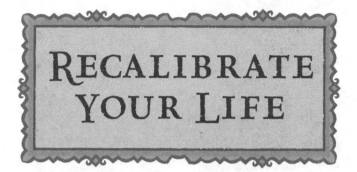

RECALIBRATE YOUR LIFE

Navigating Transitions
with Purpose & Hope

**KENNETH BOA
& JENNY ABEL**

An imprint of InterVarsity Press
Downers Grove, Illinois

InterVarsity Press
P.O. Box 1400 | Downers Grove, IL 60515-1426
ivpress.com | email@ivpress.com

InterVarsity Press® is the publishing division of InterVarsity Christian Fellowship/USA®. For more information, visit intervarsity.org.

Scripture quotations, unless otherwise noted, are from The Holy Bible, English Standard Version, copyright © 2001 by Crossway Bibles, a division of Good News Publishers. Used by permission. All rights reserved.

While any stories in this book are true, some names and identifying information may have been changed to protect the privacy of individuals.

Published in association with the literary agency of Wolgemuth & Associates.

The publisher cannot verify the accuracy or functionality of website URLs used in this book beyond the date of publication.

Cover design and image composite: Stephen Crotts
Interior design: Daniel van Loon

ISBN 978-1-5140-0072-4 (print) | ISBN 978-1-5140-0073-1 (digital)

Printed in the United States of America ♾

Library of Congress Cataloging-in-Publication Data
A catalog record for this book is available from the Library of Congress.

29   28   27   26   25   24   23 | 12   11   10   9   8   7   6   5   4   3   2   1

Ken—

To my godchildren, William and John Stewart

"Trust in the LORD with all your heart,
and do not lean on your own understanding.
In all your ways acknowledge him,
and he will make straight your paths.
Be not wise in your own eyes;
fear the LORD, and turn away from evil."
(Proverbs 3:5-7)

Jenny—

To my children, Heidi and Wesley Abel

"For nothing will be impossible with God."
(Luke 1:37)

CONTENTS

THE ROAD GOES EVER ON AND ON

The Road goes ever on and on.

BILBO BAGGINS, THE LORD OF THE RINGS

I f you're familiar with *The Lord of the Rings* or *The Hobbit* (books or films), you'll likely recall Bilbo Baggins's walking song, "The Road Goes Ever On," sung multiple times, in multiple renditions.[1] The tune is hummed not only by Bilbo but also by Gandalf and later by Bilbo's nephew, Frodo. One day, another hobbit hears Frodo singing a version of the lyrics—which Frodo apparently picked up from his uncle without even realizing it—and asks Frodo about the words. Frodo explains that he heard the song long ago and that it reminds him of Bilbo's "last years, before he went away." Frodo continues:

> [Bilbo] used often to say there was only one Road; that it was like a great river: its springs were at every doorstep, and every path was its tributary. "It's a dangerous business, Frodo, going out of your door," he used to say. "You step into the Road, and if you don't keep your feet, there is no knowing where you might be swept off to."[2]

This organic transmission of wisdom from his uncle offers a beautiful example of cross-generational influence—of journeys from two different generations lingering together and meeting for a time, and then the younger picking up the baton of the elder; the younger, in turn, passes the mantle of wisdom to others.

In the same way, those of us who follow Jesus are on a journey, a pilgrimage, to our heavenly home. As we grow older and prepare for our hand-off to the next generation, this metaphor of life as a never-ending journey may be cliché, but it also brings clarity and comfort. We are not alone, others have gone before us, and still others are coming behind us. We participate in one another's journeys. And if we are followers of Jesus, then we are all participating in one Bigger Journey—a road that goes on until it eventually joins "some larger way," as part of Bilbo's song puts it—one that is far better and more glorious than we can even imagine. Hardships and uncertainties may mark our tenancy on earth, but these are brief compared to eternity (1 Peter 5:10), and God is ultimately guiding us toward a destination free of all suffering and full of true pleasure that will never end.

As we look toward this destiny, God is ever seeking to transfer our affections and hopes from the temporal to the eternal, from that which we can see and touch to that which is unseen. We are learning to walk by faith instead of by sight, to see with spiritual eyes instead of worldly eyes (2 Corinthians 5:7, 16).

Even mature believers tend to have a diminished view of this invisible reality. Consequently, we may grow weary, disillusioned, or sorrowful (often without even realizing why). Especially when we're younger there is the temptation to get distracted—to become caught up in the day-to-day and to assume we have so much of our lives left that we can focus on eternal things *later* (even though none of us knows if there will be a *later*). As we age, there is a temptation to focus more on the past than on the future—to assume our best days are behind us and therefore to walk with "weary feet" (as one version of Bilbo's song goes) instead of pursuing God and his purposes for our lives with "eager feet" (as another verse says) until we draw our last breath.

But let's face it, whether young or old, all of us can grow distracted or weary (Isaiah 40:31); at any age we can be tempted to stop "straining forward to what lies ahead" (Philippians 3:13). If our strength is to last and our hearts are to be renewed regularly, it is God who must do it. He is the One to empower us and push us along—to invigorate our activity so it doesn't become mere busyness and to reinvigorate us when our bodies and minds begin to fail. Only when he is living in and through us are we able to pursue this path called the Christian life (Galatians 2:20).

CHANGING SCENERY ALONG THE WAY

During our earthly pilgrimages the landscape of our lives is ever changing. But sometimes the scenery changes more dramatically. Suddenly, instead of a flat, grassy plain, we find ourselves walking uphill on steep rocks, or maybe it's the other way around—we endure a long winter (emotionally or spiritually) and suddenly we break forth into a colorful springtime. This happened to me (Jenny) several years ago as I went from a long season of infertility to a long-hoped-for season of motherhood—with all its attendant joys and challenges.

> *Times of change and transition in life—and, even more importantly, our response to them—have a dramatic impact on the course of our journey and how we progress through this life.*

What happens when the scenery changes can propel us to new heights in our walks with God—or sink us. We desire to help you navigate these transitions with purpose and hope, and we'll do so through a process we call *recalibrating*.

Stop a moment and ponder: What major life transitions have *you* gone through? (When has the landscape of your life changed, and how?) What changes are you preparing for now or in the midst of?

Life transitions are as varied in type as they are in experience. We all go through them differently, just as our life journeys are all different. Here are a few examples:

+ graduating from college or graduate school
+ getting married
+ moving
+ starting a new job
+ having a child
+ quitting your job to raise (or help raise) your kids or grandkids
+ marrying off your last child (becoming an empty nester)
+ retiring

Life changes can be voluntary, like most of those just mentioned, or involuntary. The latter types of transitions, though undesirable or un-invited, are just as (if not more) impactful: suffering a major setback, disabling accident, or life-changing health incident—or being close to someone who has. Other examples include,

+ getting a divorce
+ emerging from an abusive relationship or other trauma
+ transitioning from military to civilian life
+ losing your job or facing some other career setback or disap-pointment
+ losing a loved one, such as a parent, spouse, child, or sibling
+ getting notice from your company that you're being forced to retire
+ becoming a full-time caregiver to an ailing spouse or family member

Any of these life events—including many we haven't mentioned— qualify as moments or seasons of transition. During these pivotal times, it is important to *recalibrate: to consciously process where we have been, where we are now, and where we are headed.*

LIVING WITH AN ETERNAL PERSPECTIVE

I (Ken) first became aware of the concept of recalibrating over twenty years ago through my friend Gayle Jackson. I've been doing it ever since and have benefited from the outcomes so much that I incorporate it into my mentoring and teaching. I've found that people who are willing to take the time to recalibrate—to step back and reflect on their lives at arm's length—never regret doing so.

At the heart of recalibrating is *seeing our lives from an eternal perspective*. By this we mean not only looking at our lives as they are now or even considering the full span of our relatively brief time on earth, but viewing our lives in relation to eternity. More than head knowledge this perspective is anchored in the wisdom and truths that God uses to transform us from the inside out. When we espouse and live by an eternal perspective, we will

+ align our affections and thoughts with that which God calls valuable
+ set our hope on that which endures
+ channel our actions and motivation toward the unique purpose and opportunities God places before us every day

Many of us spend significant time cultivating a better perspective on (or insight into) temporal matters: what the stock market will do next, where to move, when to retire, which social groups to join, where to take our next vacation, which job to take, which house to purchase, whether to go forward with a medical procedure, and so on. As we advance in years, we tend to become increasingly aware that these temporal things too easily slip through our fingers. We begin to think more seriously long term—*beyond* this life—and to ask questions like,

+ Does the work I do every day matter?
+ For what purpose am I storing up all these earthly possessions? Should I be giving more to God and his purposes?

✦ Am I using my time well, or am I spending too much of it on
frivolous pursuits? Should I be serving others more instead?

✦ Am I prioritizing time with family and others I love, or am I
putting them off, presuming I can make up the time for them
later?

✦ Am I ready to die? Or do I have unfinished business on earth?

✦ Is it possible to face aging, sickness, and death without fear so
they don't haunt me?

Recalibrating helps us answer these big questions. These questions
often come to the fore during transitions, though they are the questions we should be asking all along.

BEYOND SELF-HELP

To recalibrate, of course, we must have first *calibrated*. If we have never
calibrated to an eternal perspective, it's impossible to *re*-calibrate to one.
For followers of Jesus this calibration begins with knowing our new
identity in Christ. If you have never entrusted your life to Christ, or to
refresh yourself on who Christ has made you, pause right now for tool 1.

TOOL 1: ROOTING YOUR IDENTITY IN CHRIST

We must calibrate in order to recalibrate, and spiritual calibration
means aligning our minds and hearts with Jesus'. It means trusting
Christ for salvation and eternal life, and embracing the new identity he
gives us in him.

Following is a small sampling of truths about this new identity (see
more at recalibrateyourlife.org).

✦ I am a child of God (John 1:12).

✦ My old self was crucified with Christ, and I am no longer a slave
to sin (Romans 6:6).

- ✦ God leads me in triumph and the knowledge of Christ (2 Corinthians 2:14).
- ✦ I have been set free in Christ (Galatians 5:1).
- ✦ I have been blessed with every spiritual blessing in the heavenly places (Ephesians 1:3).
- ✦ I am God's workmanship created to produce good works (Ephesians 2:10).
- ✦ I am a citizen of heaven (Philippians 3:20).
- ✦ I have been made complete in Christ (Colossians 2:10).
- ✦ My life is hidden with Christ in God (Colossians 3:3).
- ✦ Christ is my life, and I will be revealed with him in glory (Colossians 3:4).

Only when we understand who Jesus is—and who we are in him—will we be secure enough to take the risks in the temporal that will lead to true, eternal gain. He enables us through spiritual wisdom to ascertain and make necessary course corrections. He moves us from one stage to the next, with the final transition being to our eternal home with him.

Without God recalibration is a dead end, an exercise in futility—boiling down to self-improvement, with no real hope or end goal beyond this life. With him, however, recalibration is more than a self-help technique. It's a distinctly Christian process that increases our focus and dependence on God; it leads to our becoming more conformed to the image of his Son and to being people he can use to reproduce his life in others.

We are recalibrating, then, for a specific purpose: to maintain or regain an eternal, Christ-centered perspective and to apply that Christ-empowered perspective in every component of our lives.

Recalibrating can be seen as a conscious response of obedience to commands like

> Therefore, my beloved . . . work out your own salvation with fear and trembling, for it is God who works in you, both to will and to work for his good pleasure. (Philippians 2:12-13)

> Do not be conformed to this world, but be transformed by the renewal of your mind, that by testing you may discern what is the will of God, what is good and acceptable and perfect. (Romans 12:2)

> Therefore, since we are surrounded by so great a cloud of witnesses, let us also lay aside every weight, and sin which clings so closely, and let us run with endurance the race that is set before us, looking to Jesus, the founder and perfecter of our faith. (Hebrews 12:1-2)

> Forgetting what lies behind and straining forward to what lies ahead, I press on toward the goal for the prize of the upward call of God in Christ Jesus. (Philippians 3:13-14)

> We look not to the things that are seen but to the things that are unseen. For the things that are seen are transient, but the things that are unseen are eternal. (2 Corinthians 4:18)

Working out our salvation, renewing our minds, running with endurance, straining forward, pressing on, looking to the things that are unseen—all of these actions focus us less and less on that which is passing away and more and more on that which is lasting and real. They anchor us in that which never changes amid lives that are ever changing.

THE ROLE OF SUFFERING

Even desirable transitions like marriage or taking a promotion at work can be difficult. This is partly because every transition involves a loss of some kind: life as it once was. "Our two sons are about to get married," reflects one father. "We've been preparing them for this. This has always been our goal—to launch them." Yet, even as he and his wife are excited for this next stage, for seeing God's plan unfold in their sons' lives, the excitement is tinged with grief. "Life will never be the same again," he says. "So there is an element of sadness alongside the happiness."

Of course, many life changes involve some form of suffering that goes beyond nostalgic sadness. With these changes the scenery of our life changes from sunny to dark. Yet, even in the most difficult transitions, viewed through the lens of eternity, we can experience joy because as followers of Jesus our joy is rooted in the unchanging character of our God and Savior, not in our circumstances. It's often in our darkest trials that *true* joy emerges. The fleeting nature of this world and its pleasures becomes more obvious, and we come to trust in and cling to Christ in ways we wouldn't have otherwise. Whether it's being diagnosed with cancer or losing a job, major changes, even when thrust unwillingly on us, have a way of stripping away the temporal things we were leaning on too much and throwing us at the feet of Jesus.

> So we do not lose heart. Though our outer self is wasting away, our inner self is being renewed day by day. For this light momentary affliction is preparing for us an eternal weight of glory beyond all comparison, as we look not to the things that are seen but to the things that are unseen. For the things that are seen are transient, but the things that are unseen are eternal. (2 Corinthians 4:16-18)

Keli endured a painful divorce after thirty years of marriage. She faced the need to process her husband's repeated unfaithfulness to her along with alienation from her kids, all while job hunting. Her path of healing and recalibration continues today. Although her life remains difficult, she presses on, her eyes trained on her eternal destiny where there will be no more pain or brokenness:

After a career of being a wife and homeschool mom, there weren't decades of career experience to fall back on to now support myself. It literally was putting one foot in front of the other, stressful, but noticing the people God put in my path and wanting to learn in each new situation. And God blessed that and has guided me through very tiresome days. . . . I understand more from where I'm standing now. God allows the hard stuff. I'm sure I've caused hardship too, and God uses that in spite of me for their growth too.

For Keli, as for all of us, God uses our suffering to shape us. The suffering isn't good in and of itself, but it can be used by God for good in our lives, spurring growth and transformation that would not occur otherwise. It's not so much the circumstances of our pain but our response to that pain that matters most.[3]

Recalibrating in the midst or aftermath of suffering can take years, as it has for Keli. In a sense it's a process that is never complete as long as we're on this earth. But we can be sure God will complete the work he has begun in us (Philippians 1:6).

Of course, ideally we don't wait for painful events in our lives to force us to recalibrate. But often it's the traumatic circumstances—the suspicious mass that shows up on an MRI, the suicide of a family member or friend—that God uses to jolt us out of the routine and prompt us to take a time-out. During these times we can survey the lay of the land, regain our bearings, and retrain our gaze on the eternal purposes of God.

TYPES OF RECALIBRATION

We've been speaking of recalibration mainly in the context of transitions or events in our lives, either voluntary or involuntary, that precipitate a revisiting of our past, present, and future. But recalibration doesn't always occur in such contexts. We can also recalibrate regularly as a part of the rhythm of our lives. We call these two kinds of recalibration *kairos* recalibration and *chronos* recalibration.

Kairos is a Greek word meaning "opportunity." *Kairos* recalibration occurs because our usual routine has been interrupted in some way—a transition has occurred or is occurring. As a result, we stop and reflect on the implications of the transition, event, or new life circumstance. For example, *kairos* recalibration could occur with the news that we are expecting our first child, with the start of a new job, after a divorce, or following the sudden death of a loved one.

Chronos, from which we get the words *chronology* and *chronograph*, refers to clock or calendar time. *Chronos* recalibration is something we schedule into our calendar, no matter what else is going on. It might occur annually, for instance, during a one-day retreat or the first weekend of January. Or we might use the occasion of our birthday to recalibrate (taking a little extra time to do so on our decade birthdays—thirty, forty, fifty, and so on—which seem to naturally provoke reflection on our lives). Married couples might choose to recalibrate together, though this shouldn't completely replace individual recalibration times.

We can think of *chronos* recalibration on several levels: micro, midi, and macro. We can recalibrate on a daily or weekly basis (micro), a monthly basis (midi), or an annual (or less frequently) basis (macro). These levels of recalibration may happen naturally and unconsciously in your life already. For instance, you might spend an hour or two every Sunday taking stock of the past week and preparing for the coming week. Or maybe you spend thirty minutes or an hour every morning getting mentally and spiritually ready for the day.

Usually, unless we schedule *chronos* recalibration into our calendars, it will not happen. It's too easy to forge full speed ahead in life, like a freight train with no brakes. Most of us put off the important in favor of the urgent, and our lives are constantly harried as a result.[4] But without taking time to process our life journey with God, not only when the scenery of our lives changes but also in the mundane sameness of daily routines, life can begin to happen *to* us. Without even realizing it, we can get swept downstream in the current, and before we know it we look around and wonder where we are, how we got there, and whether we're the same person anymore. Veering off course by one degree may have been imperceptible at the time it occurred, but over time, without a course correction, we'll end up miles off course. Righting the ship will take a lot more effort at that point. No wonder mariners recalibrate frequently on the open seas!

Here's another analogy. We can think of *kairos* and *chronos* recalibration in terms of either medical or car care. We need emergency visits because of a sudden or acute problem, but we also need regular, preventive maintenance or checkups (in fact, the latter tend to reduce the number or severity of the former). Likewise, we all need both *kairos* and *chronos* recalibration to help us stay on course and avoid mistakes and regrets in how we spent our time, energy, and resources.

As with anything worthwhile, recalibration takes intentionality, planning, and effort. But it is well worth the trouble.

My (Jenny's) transition to motherhood has been a welcome and joyful one, but not without its challenges. Before the arrival of each of our two children, my husband and I took trips to peaceful locations to consciously prepare for the coming transition (*kairos* recalibration). We asked ourselves proactive questions about how we would parent, how we would adjust and manage work responsibilities in light of our new parenting responsibilities, and how we would continue to nurture our marriage. Now, with two very young kids to care for full time, *chronos* recalibration is hard to find time for, but it's almost more necessary; without it, life moves fast, and it's easy to get caught up in the flurry of day-to-day needs while (temporarily) losing sight of an eternal perspective on the two precious souls we're now entrusted with.

No matter how busy we are, with a little intentionality and creativity, everyone can find time to recalibrate. In fact, we can't afford not to. At the same time, recalibration should not be misused. It is not a means for beating oneself up over what we aren't doing. I (Jenny) oversleep and miss times of recalibration. Both Ken and I openly concede that we do not always succeed in implementing what we planned during times of recalibration (sometimes lessons have to be learned more than once!). Thus, God and his grace must be at the center of recalibration. It's his grace that saves us, and it's his grace that grows us. Recalibration simply cannot yield lasting fruit apart from him (John 15:5).

WANTING OUR LIVES TO MATTER

At the heart of recalibrating is a deep desire for our lives to count. We want our lives to matter in a lasting manner—to be connected to that "larger way" Bilbo Baggins sang about. And it's ideal if we think in these terms early in life rather than waiting until our health is waning and our energy is dwindling to consciously process how we can spend more of our time, money, and energy on things of eternal value (relationships, ministry, our spiritual development) and less on the things that are passing away. If we assume we can make up for lost time and suddenly create a godly legacy in our later years, we make a grave mistake that ignores two important realities.

> *Our legacy starts now, and it formulates throughout our life, however long or short that may be.*

First, none of us is guaranteed another day (Psalm 90:12; James 4:13-14). We don't *know* when we're living our final days or months or years. We can make a projection based on average life expectancy data, but none of us knows if we'll be an exception to the average. Scripture is clear that we are not to presume upon the future but to take advantage of the opportunities God gives us today since we may not have tomorrow. We shouldn't wait to determine our legacy until we're older, for that day may never come.

Second, life builds on itself. We're foolish to assume we can suddenly get our act together in the last years after a lifetime of poor choices and prioritizing the wrong things. Our character and legacy build over time through the accumulation of many little decisions. Large choices certainly define us, but they do not occur in a vacuum; they are made on the basis of a matrix of smaller choices that ultimately determine our true character.

None of this is intended to discourage you if you're already in the later years of life. When the apostle Paul reflected on his own former life of persecuting the church and doing everything he could to work against Christ, he said, "But by the grace of God I am what I am, and his grace toward me was not in vain" (1 Corinthians 15:10). All of our lives, including the timing of when God works in and through us, are in his hands. When he works, no matter how old we are, his grace will be effective. We need not be filled with fear or regret, because our God can redeem or repay what the locusts have eaten (Joel 2:25). Yet this doesn't give us a free pass to live for ourselves and make poor choices earlier in our lives. God will hold us accountable for the truth and wisdom currently revealed to us. He is not a harsh master, but neither are his expectations low. He expects us to use the power and resources he has made available to us to labor heartily for him so we can say with Paul, "I labored even more than all of them, *yet not I, but the grace of God with me*" (1 Corinthians 15:10 NASB, emphasis added). Nothing good in our lives is done apart from his grace, and yet what *great* work he can do with a life surrendered to him! And he will reward those who are faithful to the opportunities and time he does give.

FINISHING WELL

If our lives are to matter in a lasting way, Scripture repeatedly emphasizes the need to persevere to the end, to press on in our faith, and to finish well (Matthew 10:22; Hebrews 3:14; 6:11).[5] In other words we're to avoid fizzling out or choking, as it's called in athletics.

If you watch a track and field race, or if you've run one yourself, you know how the competition starts. Runners burst out from their starting positions and (assuming it's not a short sprint) settle into a rhythm, pacing themselves. Toward the end (if they've trained right) they pick up their speed again and finish as strong as possible, giving every last ounce of strength they can muster as they cross the finish line. Those who haven't trained and planned ahead often run out of juice early and fizzle; they don't have any reserves to put forth that last burst of energy. They may even collapse.

The way many proceed through life is more similar to the fizzlers than the well-trained runners. Whether it's because of distraction, entanglement with sin (and refusal to repent), exhaustion, failure to plan, loss of interest, or some other reason, they succumb to the temptation to bow out of the game and bench themselves in their final years: "I deserve a rest," "I've done my part," or "I'm too old" might be how they express it. (Please note: We're *not* talking about a needed reduction in activity as a result of declining health, nor are we talking about appropriate transitions in leadership because of a recognition that it's time for us to step down and train others to step up. We're speaking of those who have chosen to disengage entirely from ministry.) The idea of a benched Christian starkly contrasts with the call of Scripture:

> We have come to share in Christ, if indeed we hold our original confidence firm to the end. (Hebrews 3:14)

> We desire each one of you to show the same earnestness to have the full assurance of hope until the end. (Hebrews 6:11)

> Let us run with endurance the race that is set before us. (Hebrews 12:1)

> Here is a call for the endurance and faith of the saints. (Revelation 13:10)

According to Paul, without diligence and recalibration we're all in danger of veering off course and fizzling in our spiritual walk. For this reason continual training from the time we first come to Christ until we draw our final breath is essential—having implications for the rest of our lives and beyond.

Do you not know that in a race all the runners run, but only one receives the prize? So run that you may obtain it. Every athlete exercises self-control in all things. They do it to receive a perishable wreath, but we an imperishable. So I do not run aimlessly; I do not box as one beating the air. But I discipline my body and keep it under control, lest after preaching to others I myself should be disqualified. (1 Corinthians 9:24-27)

Pay close attention to yourself and to your teaching; persevere in these things, for as you do this you will ensure salvation both for yourself and for those who hear you. (1 Timothy 4:16 NASB)

Notice, from Paul's words to Timothy the failure to live and finish well doesn't hurt us alone, but it hurts others as well. And despite appearances it's nearly always the result of a slow leak, not out of the blue. Small decisions of disobedience or neglect in our relationship with God accumulate little by little until character is eroded.

"A little sleep, a little slumber,
A little folding of the hands to rest,"—
Your poverty will come in like a drifter,
And your need like an armed man. (Proverbs 6:10-11 NASB)

We don't finish life well automatically or by accident. We do so when God's faithfulness to complete his work in us meets our commitment to him—through ongoing discipline and self-control—"train yourself for godliness," as Paul put it to his younger protégé (1 Timothy 4:7). We're not advocating perfectionism but a steady devotion to pursuing God and returning to him when we fail. That's what recalibration is all about: deepening intimacy with Christ, which in turn motivates you to approach more of your time, attention, and resources with the mindset that all you are and have comes from him.

RECALIBRATING: A PERSONAL PROCESS

Recalibration is a personal process that works best in the life of the person who genuinely understands God's grace—the catalyst for all genuine spiritual maturation. Ultimately, we desire that through recalibration (both the *kairos* and *chronos* kinds) you will capture a vision for the remainder of your journey on earth, however long or short that may be: a purpose- and hope-filled vision of a life in which *the best is yet to come.* That *best* may not be felt or experienced to a large extent until the next life, but it's the best because *Jesus is there.*

Practical exercises and tools form the heart of *Recalibrate Your Life* and are interspersed throughout the narrative, which generally moves from *knowing* (part one: "Perspective: What Gives Meaning to Life?") to *being* (part two: "Purpose: What Gives Direction to Life?") to *doing* (part three: "Practice: How Do I Wisely Invest My Life?"). Additional tools and an index of all tools, including some online (recalibrate yourlife.org), follow the last chapter.

We encourage you to work through the tools as you come to them in your reading. However, you may prefer to complete longer ones during a planned recalibration retreat so you aren't rushed (see tool 2). See the index for our recommendations on how often to revisit a tool. This is important because a personal purpose statement will do little good if it's never revisited after first developing it. Likewise, legacy plans need revising periodically, especially when life circumstances change.

As you encounter each tool, feel free to skip those that are irrelevant or less appealing (you can always come back to them another time). You also may want to adapt exercises to better suit your situation and style.

This process will be much more enjoyable and motivating—and you will be far more likely to follow through on action items—if you find someone else to journey alongside you. This accountability partner can be someone who reads this book at the same time as you. Small groups may also enjoy going through this book together.

Recalibrating is an immediate invitation to hit reset in your relationship with God, to get honest before him, and to rely on him more (and on your own wisdom and resources less). However this process looks for you, may it spur fresh growth in your relationship with the Lord so you will "flourish in the courts of our God" and remain "full of sap and green" every single day that the Lord has sovereignly set you on this planet (Psalm 92:13-14).

READ AND REFLECT ON
Hebrews 12:1-3

Prayer: Lord, I draw near to you, recalibrating my position so that I am fixing my eyes on you amid the ever-changing scenery of my life. People change, circumstances change, but you never change. May I lean on you, my Solid Rock. At the same time tenderize my heart and help me to be open to new things you want to do in and through me. Break up the hard soil that may have formed, and make way for new growth and life. Amen.

TOOL 2: GUIDE TO A PERSONAL RECALIBRATION RETREAT

To ensure our focus is on the eternal and we are stewarding our time and opportunities wisely here on earth, it is helpful if we recalibrate both at moments of transition (*kairos* recalibration) and on a regular basis (*chronos* recalibration). *Chronos* recalibration helps us approach our lives with intentionality rather than simply reacting as life happens to us. *Kairos* recalibration, on the other hand, turns an event, either anticipated or unanticipated (such as getting married, having a child, retiring, or receiving a difficult medical diagnosis), into an opportunity for personal spiritual growth as we consider the implications of our changed circumstances. Both types of recalibration help us recognize when we need to make midcourse adjustments and enable us to be proactive with all that God has given us (even the trials) so that we make the greatest possible impact for his everlasting kingdom.

Following is a possible outline for an annual recalibration retreat. Adapt as you wish!

ANNUAL CHRONOS RECALIBRATION

Prepare

Plan a one-day or half-day retreat, placing it on your calendar like any other appointment, as far in advance as possible. Do this annually (e.g., on a particular day each year or around your birthday).

Choose a setting away from noise and distractions, preferably one surrounded by nature, where the only noises you hear are the wind, birds, and insects.

Leave electronics at home. If you must bring them, turn them off and do not check them except for an emergency.

Take a journal or notebook, a writing utensil, and a Bible.

Retreat

We recommend you spend from half an hour to two hours on each of the following four steps.

1. Backward look. Remember and reflect on the story God is writing into your life. Realize that he can use every single part of it—every event, job, relationship, and even the hardships, setbacks, and mistakes—for a redemptive purpose.

Whole-life review. Consider taking your life in five- or ten-year increments, reviewing key people, activities and achievements, challenges, and insights from each. Record them in your journal/notebook. Then, synthesize what you noted by jotting down any patterns and common themes. Finally, in a few sentences summarize the trajectory your life has taken up until this point.

One-year review. Review key events, key changes, and key relationships from the past year. What is new or different from a year ago?

What has stayed the same? What are you thankful for? What regrets do you have? What difficulties have you encountered?

2. *Upward look.* Spend time connecting with God through prayer and his Word. Focus on *being* (in his presence) rather than *doing* during this time.

Possible focus Scriptures: Psalm 90; Psalm 102; Psalm 145; 2 Corinthians 4:16-18; Hebrews 13:8.

Seek a balanced time of prayer, beginning with thanksgiving and adoration, followed by confession of sin and renewal. Next, make supplication (requests), first for yourself (petition) and then for others (intercession). End with an affirmation of God's will and ask for an open and discerning heart and mind as you continue with the rest of your retreat.

3. *Inward look.* Prayerfully conduct an honest self-assessment or seek steps toward personal growth (e.g., by completing one or more of the tools in this book).

Consider using "Seven Keys to Living and Finishing Well" (see appendix).

4. *Forward look.* Look to the future and determine needed adjustments—allowing your destination to define your journey.

✦ How do you want your life to be different
- in one year?
- in five years?

✦ How will you get there? Consider the following areas and prayerfully come up with two to three actionable goals.

- What character traits do you need to work on?
- What values do you need to embrace more? (See tool 5 for ideas.)
- What activities do you need to start (or stop) doing, or do differently?
- How should you implement each of these changes?
- What barriers might you encounter that you can plan for?

- Do you have a reliable recalibration (accountability) partner? When will you plan to discuss this retreat with that person?

Kairos Recalibration

Follow the same basic outline as for *chronos* recalibration for positive or painful events in your life, with the following adjustments.

1. Backward look. Instead of a whole-life or one-year review, conduct a review of your current transition or recent event that prompted you to recalibrate. What happened (or is happening)? What are the things that led up to this point? What has changed? How does this fit within the larger context of your life?

2. Upward look. Take the issue of concern (the event or transition) to the Lord. Ask him to search you and know you on this matter (Psalm 139:23-24) and to give you humility and openness to see it from his perspective and to receive his wisdom as you move forward.

3. Inward look. Conduct an honest self-assessment on this particular event or transition. How is it affecting you? How is it influencing your outlook?

4. Forward look. How can you move forward with an eternal perspective on this event or transition? Are there any specific actions you need to take (e.g., extending forgiveness to someone, prayerfully putting personal boundaries in place, seeking a sage you can go to for wise advice, or joining in fellowship or prayer with others in a similar situation)?

PART I

PERSPECTIVE

*What Gives
Meaning to Life?*

CHAPTER ONE

LEAVING A
GODLY LEGACY

As for man, his days are like grass;
he flourishes like a flower of the field;
for the wind passes over it, and it is gone,
and its place knows it no more.
But the steadfast love of the LORD is from everlasting
to everlasting on those who fear him.

PSALM 103:15-17

I (Ken) have had sixteen near-death experiences—these are, of course, the ones I know about. My first was a near-drowning experience at age thirteen. I swam out too far in a North Jersey lake and couldn't get myself back in. I began to slip under the water. After going under for the third time, I felt a hand pull me up even though no one had been around, and suddenly I found myself on shore. To this day I don't know who pulled me out of the water. I didn't have a relationship with Jesus at the time, so the incident certainly got my attention.

In those moments time often dilated for me, my entire life flashing before my eyes. I was suddenly aware that I am, like every other person on this planet, living on borrowed time.

These types of fear-inducing moments can help crystallize for us what God is trying to teach us every day. Life is brief. Life is fragile. Every day is precious; don't waste it. Tomorrow isn't guaranteed to anyone. *Live each day as though it could be the last.*

TOOL 3: ONE YEAR TO LIVE

Brushes with death—whether a near-drowning experience in your teenage years, a cancer diagnosis in your thirties, a heart attack in your fifties, or a life-threatening fall in your seventies—have a way of forcing us to ask the important questions that we should have been asking all along. They cause us to pause and reflect on whether we're spending our lives well. Take a moment to think over the following questions and then ask God to help you live in light of the answers.

✦ If you found out you only have one year to live, how would you spend your time and your resources (money, other assets) differently?

✦ If you found out you only have one year to live, what would you be leaving behind? Think in terms of both tangibles and intangibles.

✦ In light of your answers, consider,

- How do you want to be remembered?
- What course corrections should you make to ensure you're living every year (and day) as though it's your last?

Note: This exercise is not intended to discourage future planning or long-term pursuits! We all do well to live as though we have a year left, but plan as though we have more.

THE NEXT GENERATIONS AND THE BREVITY OF LIFE

Moses captured the transitory nature of human life in Psalm 90:

> Teach us to number our days
> that we may get a heart of wisdom. (Psalm 90:12)

In this oldest of the psalms, the only one written by Moses, we have the perspective of a wise and godly man looking back on his journey at the end of a long life. At first, he recalls God's faithfulness across times and epochs:

> Lord, you have been our dwelling place
> in all generations.
> Before the mountains were brought forth,
> or ever you had formed the earth and the world,
> from everlasting to everlasting you are God.
> (Psalm 90:1-2)

Moses, by this point in his life, had the wisdom to know we should never live presumptuously but should live in expectation of the Spirit of God working in our lives; he had seen God do so repeatedly, rescuing his children in the wilderness even when they did not deserve it. He contrasts the nature of the *everlasting* God with human life, which is fleeting and returns to dust (Psalm 90:3).

Moses continues with a perspective on time. A millennium feels long from a human point of view, but for God it's like a day—a blip on the timeline of eternity. Moses then uses two metaphors to drive home the brevity of life:

> You sweep them [generations] away as with a flood; they are
> like a dream,
> like grass that is renewed in the morning:
> in the morning it flourishes and is renewed;
> in the evening it fades and withers. (Psalm 90:5-6)

The mindset is this: a generation comes, builds its buildings, and achieves some feats. But as soon as everything is built (sometimes even before the work is finished), it's as though a flood comes and washes it all away. Using another analogy, Moses says each generation is like grass—sprouting anew one day, withered and gone the next.

A. W. Tozer gives a similar metaphor in *The Knowledge of the Holy*, drawing from a verse in the book of Job. "The days of the years of our lives are few, and swifter than a weaver's shuttle. Life is a short and fevered rehearsal for a concert we cannot stay to give. Just when we appear to have attained some proficiency we are forced to lay our instruments down."[1]

Have you seen weavers working a loom? They take the shuttle and shoot it across the loom, then down. This was a brilliant way of fast-forwarding long before such technology existed. The analogy is that of one day after another whizzing past, and before you know it, the weaving is complete.

Such is the nature of life.

If you've ever stood on the ocean shore observing the tide, you'll catch the vision that both Moses and Tozer are communicating. Humans and all their earthly achievements are like those huge, grand sandcastles—impressive for a moment, but as soon as the tide comes in, they're swept along with whatever other rubble surrounded them—seaweed, shells, dead jellyfish, ocean debris. Before long you'd never know any of it was there. All that's left is the foundation.

The question we all wonder is, *Am I building sandcastles that will be knocked down and forgotten forever once I die?* In other words, *Am I writing my name on water?* Or am I living in a way that will make a permanent mark? Is there a sure foundation I can build on—something I can do or be that will never get swept away?

Scripture contends that our lives *do* matter, not only collectively but individually, and that each of us can serve as a link from one generation to the next. In other words we can leave a positive, godly legacy that makes an eternal imprint. And we need not wait to begin building this legacy.

LEGACY FROM GOD'S STANDPOINT

The Bible speaks of "legacy" using terms such as *inheritance, offspring, generations,* and *descendants.* Some of the most poignant passages about what it means to live and leave a godly legacy are found in the psalms. In Psalm 145, for example, the psalmist (David) writes:

> One generation shall commend your works to another,
> and shall declare your mighty acts.
> On the glorious splendor of your majesty,
> and on your wondrous works, I will meditate.
> They shall speak of the might of your awesome deeds,
> and I will declare your greatness.
> They shall pour forth the fame of your abundant goodness
> and shall sing aloud of your righteousness.
> (Psalm 145:4-7)

The following passage bears a similar sentiment:

> O God, from my youth you have taught me,
> and I still proclaim your wondrous deeds.
> So even to old age and gray hairs,
> O God, do not forsake me,
> until I proclaim your might to another generation,
> your power to all those to come. (Psalm 71:17-18)[2]

Psalm 78, attributed to Asaph, focuses almost exclusively on the coming generation. Notice the warning to those who forget God and refuse to repent and live for him:

> He made their days vanish like a breath,
> and their years in terror. (Psalm 78:33)

The lives of these unfaithful people are not only fleeting but end "in terror." Moreover, the work they accomplished during their earthly sojourns has no lasting meaning—it's utterly destroyed:

> He gave their crops to the destroying locust
> and the fruit of their labor to the locust. (Psalm 78:46)

Of course, all crops and livestock die eventually, but the point is symbolic. The final verdict of their work represents the opposite of what Moses prays for:

> Let the favor of the Lord our God be upon us,
> and establish the work of our hands upon us;
> yes, establish the work of our hands! (Psalm 90:17)

Here, we see the first important truth that we must grab hold of if any of us is to have any kind of lasting legacy: *it is God who gives us a legacy.* He establishes our work (here, we're referring to *work* in a broad sense) and makes it meaningful. Try as we might to establish our own legacies, the blessing of having our lives count from a kingdom standpoint is his to determine.

A second important truth about legacy is closely related to the first. *Legacy from a biblical standpoint is about God, not us.* If our primary concern is that *we* are remembered, we've missed the point of life. Psalm 45 teaches us instead that perpetuating God's name is what counts—and it's what makes *our lives* count:

> I will cause your name to be remembered in all generations;
> therefore nations will praise you forever and ever.
> (Psalm 45:17)

This prayer echoes the spirit of Psalm 145. Notice that passage (145:4-7) focuses on God, not on us. While his people are given the privilege of living forever in his presence, the key to legacy on earth is a desire to honor the Creator, who binds every generation together. Take a look at the content of this legacy from Psalm 145:4-7 in table 2.1.

Table 2.1. Content of a godly legacy

How (command/verb)	What
commend/praise	God's works
declare	his mighty acts
meditate	his majesty, his wondrous works
speak	the might of his awesome deeds
declare/tell	his greatness
pour forth/eagerly utter	his abundant goodness
sing aloud/shout joyfully	his righteousness
(Words taken from ESV and NASB)	

How we accomplish what David prays in Psalm 145 will be distinctive to each of our lives and contexts.

SELF- OR CHRIST-EXALTING?

Luke, a recent college graduate, isn't yet sure what the content of his legacy will be, but he understands the one who will establish it.

"I first started thinking about legacy after watching *National Treasure: Book of Secrets*," Luke explains. "The villain in that movie chose to give up his life to make his 'mark on history'; to him it was the only thing that mattered in the end. It got the thought rolling around in my head: Who's going to remember me? What are they going to remember me for?"

Though raised in a Christian family, Luke underwent a transformation in his early twenties. Having known the gospel for years, the faith of his parents was finally made real to him.

"After spending a lot of time pursuing self-importance, God broke into my heart and shuffled around my thoughts on legacy," Luke says. "I can leave a legacy now by making my business the pursuit of Christ. Can I be more like him today? That's the real question of legacy now. Let him take me to glorious places or keep me out of the limelight. Either way I know I'm spending my life the best way I possibly can."

Although Luke, like many people his age, says he isn't yet sure what he wants to do with his life, as a student of the Word who hungers for the wisdom of older mentors and guides, and who isn't preoccupied with his own sense of significance, he is positioned better than most of his peers to discern the unique purpose God has created him for. And in an age of selfies and social media, his spurning of self-exaltation is certainly admirable and unusual.

Luke's mindset contrasts starkly with the king's in Percy Bysshe Shelley's poem "Ozymandias," whose lasting mark was a pedestal containing these words:

> My name is Ozymandias, King of Kings;
> Look on my Works, ye Mighty, and despair!
> Nothing beside remains. Round the decay
> Of that colossal Wreck, boundless and bare
> The lone and level sands stretch far away.

Focused on making a name for himself, Ozymandias epitomized what he tried so hard *not* to become: a shattered statue, lifeless and devoid of glory. The poet's words contrast starkly with those of the psalmist's:

> The righteous flourish like the palm tree
>   and grow like a cedar in Lebanon.
> They are planted in the house of the LORD;
>   they flourish in the courts of our God.
> They still bear fruit in old age;
>   they are ever full of sap and green,
> to declare that the LORD is upright;
>   he is my rock, and there is no unrighteousness in him.
>   (Psalm 92:12-15)

Crumbling, lifeless stone or an ever-living, verdant tree? As Luke expressed so well, we can pursue self-importance or Christlikeness, self-exaltation or Christ exaltation. Our choice determines our final legacy.

Make no mistake, God honors the individual; we're not lost in a sea of collectivity. But ultimately, all points to him, and a preoccupation with preserving our own memory, for our own sake and name, is not scriptural. Instead, for those who follow and love God, he promises to establish us, our work, and our purpose—for *his* name's sake.

WHAT ABOUT CHILDREN AND GRANDCHILDREN?

If you ask people what their plans are for their retirement years, those who have a plan almost always mention family—especially children and grandchildren. Investing in the next generation provides one of the greatest senses of satisfaction and lasting significance. And yet even *this* can have only a fleeting impact if it is not done with a God-centered focus and purpose.

When I (Jenny) struggled for over a decade with infertility, one of the concerns I had related to inheritance. The question wasn't just who gets all our stuff after we die (although for items like photographs and journals, I certainly mulled that over periodically). There was also an innate desire for not only my physical DNA but the spiritual and moral DNA of my life, of our family, to be continued. Who would be the recipient of these things if I never had children? Most of us never consider how this very honest, human question might preoccupy those who remain single or childless.

Offspring in the Bible are a good and godly desire (Psalm 127:3-5). Paul goes so far as to say that if we don't take care of our relatives, we have effectively "denied the faith" and are "worse than an unbeliever" (1 Timothy 5:8).

To be sure, we're commanded to be fruitful and multiply biologically speaking. But legacy, according to the Bible, goes beyond DNA and blood relations.

God promised to bless the entire world through descendants of Abraham, many of whom would not be directly related by blood to him. The Jewish rulers often fell into the same trap we do, thinking that biological relations are what matter. No wonder they were so confused by Jesus' words recorded in the Gospel of Matthew: "Do not presume to say to yourselves, 'We have Abraham as our father'; for I tell you, God is able from these stones to raise children for Abraham" (Matthew 3:9).

Throughout Jesus' ministry the truth became clear: God is not concerned with DNA-based legacy (bloodline inheritance). He is concerned with those who are spiritual children of Abraham—that is, children of the promise he made to Abraham (Romans 9:8).

When we think of legacy and inheritance, we must have this expanded, scriptural view as well. Psalm 145 never says that our acts of declaring, praising, and singing of God to the next generation *have* to be done toward children we call our own (biological or adopted). Of course, if we have them, we should do so (1 Timothy 5:8). But our legacy shouldn't stop there. And if we don't have earthly progeny, we can still fully answer God's call to bear lasting fruit.

The question is this:

> *Who are you investing in to ensure that the works*
> *of God, the goodness of God, and the faithfulness of*
> *God are passed on to the next generation?*

It might be young neighbors, children of friends, the kids in the nursery at church, the young people at the school or college down the road, or the members of the baseball team you coach. It might not even be young people directly—you might be a teacher or mentor or encourager to others who are training the next generation. Or you might be writing books that have an impact on both the current and next generations. The possibilities of spiritual fruitfulness and legacy are endless, and they go far beyond biology.

Consider Andrea. She never married or had children. After more than three decades as an administrator with a large department store, she keenly felt the changed (slower) pace that retirement brought.

With "so little to do compared to when I was working," and knowing she "wasn't doing [herself] any favors by becoming a total couch potato," she joined a gym and began exercising several times a week with a trainer (despite being "*very* sedentary" throughout her life). The workouts, however, did more harm than good, and she was soon dealing with crippling pain. Now recovered, she looks back and realizes the experience was one way God was shifting her focus more toward him in her later years. Her attention turned from frantically trying to get fit and lose some pounds to "enjoying doing whatever the Lord gives [her] to do and becoming the woman he created [her] to be." Although she still walks for exercise, she is pursuing a more balanced, "reasonable" (for her) schedule of activities that focuses on God instead of herself.

"There's an old poem that begins, 'Grow old along with me. The best is yet to be—the last of life for which the first was made,'" Andrea quotes. "Although I haven't had a spouse with whom to grow old, I value my brother's family and my close friends who are like sisters, and [I] want to be the example and encourager they need." In addition to investing in extended family, she leads the music ministry at her church, is part of the teaching team for her church's women's Bible study, and sings with a statewide choir.

"After I retired," Andrea reflects,

I had to relearn how to thank him for every moment, the many quiet ones and the less-frequent busy ones, and even for the physical pain. I pray that my brother and his wife, my nephew and niece and their families, my friends and congregation will remember me as a woman who loved God and them above all else, a woman devoted to God's Word and to prayer. I'm not rich in this world's goods, so I'll have little to leave them otherwise. I want to be remembered as one who was content with the life she lived in the flesh—a life lived by the grace of God who loved me and gave himself for me.

Andrea's desire and example may seem unimpressive, ordinary. Who will ever know her impact besides the few in her circle of influence? But this is a worldly perspective that overlooks the beauty of such a life. Rest assured, in God's kingdom her ministry will not be overlooked. Hers is like the heart of the woman who spent all the wealth she had to anoint Jesus' feet with oil, and about whom the Lord said, "wherever the gospel is proclaimed in the whole world, what she has done will also be told in memory of her" (Matthew 26:13). Andrea's quiet but joyful perseverance in obeying God's call to "work out [her] own salvation with fear and trembling" (Philippians 2:12) to the very end of her earthly pilgrimage is the kind of legacy Scripture calls us to leave behind. It's a legacy that may go unrecognized and hidden to the world but will be celebrated by the Father and multiplied in its impact on his kingdom.

Human pride desires to be recognized by people and assured of the significance and results of our actions; the humble person desires that others remember God and honor *his* name because of how they lived.

Tool 4: Creating a Legacy Journal, Document, or Other Record

There is an incredible array of possibilities for passing along messages to others when you leave this earth, and many of them require some planning and effort. For example, I (Jenny) began journaling for each of my children shortly after they were born, and I plan to give these journals to them when they are older. Many people keep legacy boxes that they plan to leave to their children, and these are easiest to compile along the way so you aren't scrambling later in life to track down special items.

Following are just a few examples, which range from the personal and subjective to the more formal and objective. We encourage you to think through your style and life situation to determine which method(s) you'd like to use to communicate a life legacy message.

+ a prayer journal (recording requests and how God answered)
+ a personal diary or journal (recording your reactions to, reflections on, or prayers related to everyday living, important milestones, or key events or periods of your life)
+ life letters to loved ones—personalized messages to individuals, such as a spouse or child (see tool 17)
+ a collection of letters (rather than a single life letter, you can write to a particular person regularly across your lifetime and then instruct for the letters to be handed over to the intended recipient in a special box or packaging after or just before you die)
+ a collection of family stories (documenting family lore from your own life as well as generations before yours)
+ a faith journey document (ranging in length from a summary to a book, this can discuss your conversion as well as your testimony after God brought you to the faith)
+ a biographical profile (including professional and personal highlights)
+ a legacy statement/message (a record of what you want others to learn from your life or what you hope to pass on to the next generation)
+ a visual/multimedia legacy (a DVD, slideshow, or similar presentation that uses photographs, audio, or video recordings to communicate your love and legacy)
+ a legacy box (including any of the previous written documents but would also include special objects, mementos, news clippings, postcards, or letters you've received, stories or books you've written, and any other items that have meaning to you;

hint: be sure to label or create an index to tell where each item came from and why it's significant)

Need help getting started? Numerous services exist to aid people with the compilation of legacy documents. Two examples are Story-Worth (welcome.storyworth.com) and StoryCorps (storycorps.org). These make wonderful gifts for children and grandchildren.

DON'T WAIT OR THINK IT'S TOO LATE

As we think about legacy, we can make several mistakes. One (as just discussed) is to overemphasize our biological progeny as the recipients of our legacy. Another is to overemphasize material belongings, thinking only in terms of wills and estates, especially finances and physical assets. A third mistake relates to age and time.

When we're younger, we tend to overemphasize the future—thinking we'll get around to doing the things that matter and will make a long-term impact later, after we're done with the more urgent business of working to make money, support ourselves and our family, and so on. Elizabeth, a single twentysomething, expressed this tendency this way:

> Even though cognitively I know that I'm leaving a legacy now, I often feel like I'm being prepared to leave a legacy. . . . I can't shake the sensation that I'm waiting for something to happen at which point I will start leaving my actual legacy and living my actual life. But I don't really know what snap I'm waiting for!

Our legacy on earth has already begun (see introduction); it is not built later in life but throughout our lives, every single day, based on how we spend our time, talent, and other resources. We aren't *preparing* to leave a legacy; we're doing so already.

As a result the father who chooses to spend a little less time at the office and a little more time at home while the kids are still young makes a wise sacrifice. Likewise, the young single woman who invests spare time that she has now (and may *not* have later if and when she marries) is building her legacy as she mentors young girls struggling with self-image and helps them see their worth and value in Christ. The college students who work as Christian camp counselors over the summer are reaching youth in ways that older adults might not be able to; they too are contributing to their legacy. These are but three examples. Bottom line:

> *Legacy isn't just for later.*

On the flip side, as we age we can tend to underestimate our older selves and think *our best years are behind us*. While our health and physical vitality may wane and our circle of influence may shrink, the greatest opportunity to make an impact on the next generations can come toward the end of life. In large part this is because in our later years we tend to have

+ more free (flexible) time
+ morc resources (tangible and human ones)
+ greater wisdom and skills (the kind that comes only from experience)

Of course, these are not universally true, but they are general trends. And if we are wise, we will seize the uniqueness of the season called old age and spend it on the things that truly matter. This doesn't mean we never play golf, take a trip, pursue pleasures, or even spoil the kids and grandkids. Hear us clearly when we say there is nothing necessarily wrong with taking time to golf, helping a grandchild pay for college or even spoiling them a little, or traveling the globe.

It truly is never too early nor too late to leave a lasting legacy.

RECALIBRATING

Each of us is on earth for a purpose, and God is the one who establishes our legacy. To truly have a lasting impact we need to continually recalibrate our perspective of our time (whether we have decades or days left to live) and our resources (tangible and intangible) so that we are living in light of eternity.

Whether we are still running marathons or are severely limited physically, even bedridden, God wants to use each of us to make a lasting impact. In his economy it's not about quantity but quality, trusting that he has the power to multiply the effect of any small effort made with an attitude of submission to him. In this vein, whether we are young or old, asking endgame questions about all our activities can help ensure we will leave a godly legacy rather than pursue our own comfort or fame:

✦ Why am I doing this?

✦ Is there some other way God is calling me to spend my time, effort, or money?

✦ Is there any way I can do this same activity but with more of a God-centered focus?

✦ Am I loving God and others in this?

We need humility when answering these questions. We must be willing to make adjustments, to remain teachable and supple at all times. So many succumb to a hardening of the categories, a worse disease than the hardening of the arteries. With this condition a person becomes nearly immune to any change of thought process or life approach as they age. But no matter how much we think we know, we always have more to learn! God is always taking us even deeper and will use our pursuit of him in ways we don't always see or understand. We do both ourselves and others a disservice if we drop out of the game and sideline ourselves at any point. Our most effective time of ministry can come at any stage of our lives, for God is not constricted in the ways we are.

We encourage you to pause and take at least one concrete step toward leaving a godly legacy. Here are three ideas:

✦ Prayerfully review tool 4 and decide on an action item from it.

✦ Find a younger (less mature) brother or sister in the faith to invest in and encourage—someone God has placed in your path who may already look to you as an example or role model (see Ephesians 6:4; Colossians 3:16; Hebrews 10:24; Titus 2:1-14). Commit to regularly spending time with that person.

✦ Review tool 5. Which practices or principles is God prompting you to focus on? Which do you want to pass on to the next generation? Choose one from each category (three total) and pray for God's help in those areas. These principles and values are part of your legacy.

READ AND REFLECT ON

Psalm 145

Consider memorizing verses 4, 18

Prayer: Lord, help me to know you have created me for a purpose, you love me, and you want to use me to proclaim your name and goodness throughout the world and down through the generations. You will establish the work of my hands when I submit it to you—this is my legacy. May I never take for granted a single day in which you've given me life and breath, and may you give me the grace to respond to your loving overtures and guidance with joyful obedience and trust. Amen.

TOOL 5: PRINCIPLES AND VALUES TO LIVE BY

Following is a list of thirty-six personal principles and values to live by.[3] They provide the basis for a powerful, godly legacy. We recommend you choose one principle or value per category (three total) to focus on at a time (e.g., monthly). The goal is to help you integrate your life in Christ with your life in the world. For further edification see the expanded version of this tool online (recalibrateyourlife.org), which provides brief explanations of each principle or value along with Scripture passages for reading and meditation.

Two Important Cautions

1. Do not try to focus on all or even many of these principles or values at once (that would be overwhelming).

2. Do not use these principles as a whip or club to beat yourself up when you fall short (as we all do). No one can fully attain these ideals; they are intended as an inspirational target to aim for.

Pursue God

✦ Grow in faith.

✦ Hold fast to hope.

✦ Deepen your love for God.

✦ Value the eternal over the temporal.

✦ Grow in grace.

✦ Commit to the centrality of Christ.

✦ Remember your deepest needs are met in Christ.

✦ Practice God's presence.

✦ Seek fresh bread (don't live on yesterday's faith).

✦ Cultivate a seeing eye (looking for the glory of God in the natural world).

✦ Invite the friendship and nearness of God.

✦ Abide in the Son.

Pursue Godly Character

✦ Cultivate a spirit of humility and teachability.

✦ Live with a stewardship mindset (i.e., all we have is God's).

- Commit to the ongoing exercise and renewal of spirit, soul, and body.
- Seek personal integrity (congruence between the inside and the outside).
- Stand firm in spiritual warfare (by submitting to God first).
- Obey God to avoid living with regret.
- Choose gratitude and joy.
- Live as a pilgrim.
- Be aware that good and evil both increase at compound interest.
- Be shaped by the Word, not the world.
- Develop habits of holiness.
- Live with two days on the calendar: today and *that* Day.

Pursue the Highest Good of Others

- Commit to the second Great Commandment.
- Live with a radical commitment to the Great Commission.
- Rely on the Holy Spirit.
- Treat people better than they deserve.
- Cultivate compassion for the least, the last, and the lost.
- Be quick to forgive.
- Commit to openness and honesty in relationships.
- Let your intimacy with Christ animate your activity.
- Leave results to God.
- Resist comparison (the enemy of contentment).
- Look for *kairos* moments (God's loving initiatives that may at first appear as interruptions).
- Encourage, exhort, and edify other believers.

CHAPTER TWO

NUMBERING YOUR DAYS

Teach us to number our days
that we may get a heart of wisdom.

PSALM 90:12

ooking through old photographs of my (Ken's) wife's family, I barely recognize any of the faces other than her parents, aunts and uncles, and cousins. These are people not far removed from my own life, once very significant in the lives of those I knew and loved, and yet they've passed on and might as well be unrelated to anyone I have known. This experience always reminds me afresh of the fragility of life and our earthbound associations.

A cemetery has a similar effect: dozens of names, the details of their stories anonymous to me, accompanied only by a date range and maybe a short epitaph. The small dash between birth and death years is approximately the same length for everyone, reinforcing the fact that whether our lives are two months or eighty years long, they're all short in the grand scope of eternity.

There's an elephant in the room when we talk about legacy: death. Life is brief. Our bodies don't last forever. Our "earthly tents" are eventually destroyed, as Paul put it (2 Corinthians 5:1 NIV). And although some friends and family members will remember us after we die, eventually those people die too, and the vast majority of us wind up as ciphers, footnotes, in the annals of human history. Even those who attain a measure of fame meet this end; only a select few have names like Abraham, Isaac, and Jacob that truly carry down through the ages. And even that measure of fame is fleeting compared to eternity.

DEATH AS A PORTAL

All of us have some fear when we think about death. Scripture describes death as the "king of terrors" (Job 18:14), and indeed, if we do not have a relationship with Christ, then physical death is rightly feared, for it signifies a much worse fate: spiritual death. Both irreversible and eternal, spiritual death refers not to extinction but to separation from the One who made us for himself. In this case death is a gateway not to eternal life but to eternal misery—hence, this is why attending a nonbeliever's funeral is one of the most depressing things in the world.

Of course, some of our fears surrounding death are related not so much to what we will experience afterward but to the *process* of dying. Our concern may also be more existential: the fear of being forgotten forever after we die. There's a famous quote attributed to Woody Allen: "I don't want to achieve immortality through my work; I want to achieve immortality through not dying. Rather than live on in the hearts and minds of my fellow man, I would rather live on in my apartment."[1] We yearn for *real* immortality, not metaphorical immortality (e.g., in others' minds and imaginations or in art or architecture or other earthly achievements). Scripture suggests this longing is wired into humans: "he has put eternity into man's heart" (Ecclesiastes 3:11).

For a follower of Christ, not only do we avoid spiritual death, but these deepest longings of our hearts are fulfilled—though not in the way Woody Allen wished (and we should be glad of that). Awaiting us is a permanent home with the Father, and although we don't completely understand what it will be like, we know it is real and not merely figurative. It's a more exquisite, beautiful place than we can even fathom. We have God's solemn promise that he has prepared this place for us (John 14:2-3), though it isn't visible to us now.

So death is not the end for the follower of Christ but a portal to the beginning of a new and better life; a magnificent future awaits us. When we are freed from our bondage to sin by placing our trust in Christ, our bondage to the fear of death is also broken, and we can live with true freedom.

> Since therefore the children share in flesh and blood, he himself [Jesus] likewise partook of the same things, that through death he might destroy the one who has the power of death, that is, the devil, and deliver all those who through fear of death were subject to lifelong slavery. (Hebrews 2:14-15)

Most of us can't quite shake the discomfort or sorrow we feel about the prospect that our lives on earth will end someday. But coming to grips with our mortality is a crucial aspect of recalibrating.

A Crisis of Mortality

The older we get, the more we tend to think about the fact that our time on earth will one day end. "I used to know that the grave is on the other side of the (proverbial) hill," the saying goes, "but now I can see the darn thing!" It's not that we suddenly become more morbid in our thoughts but that reality tends to hit us—*really* hit us—harder and more frequently. Rather than seeming far off, death becomes like that crescendo of a fast-approaching train—louder and louder, with nothing stopping it no matter how hard we try to block out the sound.

> *The coffin becomes an evangelist, speaking to*
> *us more eloquently than the cradle.*

For years people have referred to the midlife crisis, usually occurring around our midforties or a little later. The term refers to an existential awareness of the brevity of our earthly sojourn. Of course, this realization never dawns on us just once but gradually throughout our lives. At certain points the awareness becomes suddenly more acute, for example when a loved one dies or we receive a serious medical diagnosis or health scare (or someone close to us does). Because the crisis can occur at any point in our life, it might be better labeled a "crisis of mortality." The crisis can be brought on by external factors, but it can also be internally prompted. We might look in the mirror one day and notice that first strand of gray hair or that first sign of a wrinkle, and it begins to preoccupy us, *I'm not going to live forever (on earth)*. Or we might experience a wave of nostalgia that drives home the fact that we're not getting younger, and time is passing faster than we'd like.

Some scholars question the existence of a midlife crisis. Work by labor economists in the 1990s led to a new philosophy about midlife: the U-shaped happiness curve. Summarizing this research, Jonathan Rauch (writing for *The Atlantic*) explains:

> [The economists discovered a] recurrent pattern in countries around the world. "Whatever sets of data you looked at," [Dartmouth College labor economist David] Blanchflower told me in a recent interview, "you got the same things": Life satisfaction would decline with age for the first couple of decades of adulthood, bottom out somewhere in the 40s or early 50s, and then, until the very last years, increase with age, often (though not always) reaching a higher level than in young adulthood. The pattern came to be known as the happiness U-curve.[2]

Rauch goes on to note that the "exact shape of the curve, and the age when it bottoms out, vary." In addition, the U-curve does not mean a person cannot be happy at midlife—just that it's "harder."[3]

Whether it happens at sixteen or sixty, even scholars skeptical of the term *midlife crisis* don't deny that nearly everyone experiences some type of crisis (or several of them) at some point in life, during which we realize the brevity of life more personally and acutely than before. Interestingly, studies of the midlife period consistently document differences between what prompts such a crisis in men versus in women. Generally speaking, for men the crisis and ensuing reevaluation of priorities tend to center around work and career. For women the crisis tends to be more internally prompted (brought on by biological and hormonal changes or family changes).

This crisis of mortality can lead to several places. First is a therapeutic, this-world approach that ultimately boils down to denial. We may still use the language of meaning and purpose, but if we are not anchored in a sure and eternal foundation (that is, the God of the Bible), even purportedly purposeful lives have no lasting purpose. Denial will only get us so far.

A second approach to our mortality is escapism. We can employ an impressive array of tactics when facing our death: distraction, feigned indifference, selective attention. We've all known the guy who impulsively runs out and buys the shiny new sports car in his fifties (maybe you're that guy). Some people find a new romantic partner. Yet sooner or later reality catches up to us all. Setbacks and afflictions that come with the aging process reveal our tactics for what they are. Regret and disillusionment creep in, and we're forced to face the inevitable.

There's a third, better way instead of denial or escapism: the pursuit of godly wisdom and spiritual maturity. That's what numbering our days is all about (Psalm 90:12). The words of Solomon capture the spirit of this approach:

> It is better to go to the house of mourning
>> than to go to the house of feasting,
> for this is the end of all mankind,
>> and the living will lay it to heart. (Ecclesiastes 7:2)

This verse isn't suggesting that we never have a good time or a large meal; rather, it is pointing to the need for us to awaken to the solemn reality of our life's fleetingness. We humans tend to be myopic, and our shortsighted souls need reminders of our status as pilgrims traveling through a temporal arena on our way to an eternal home so we don't get caught up in momentary pleasures and fail to plan for the next life. Usually, the occasion of a funeral will accomplish this much better than a celebration.

WHAT DO WE FEAR MOST?

Every person lives with a primary fear object. That ultimate fear is often wrongly placed; we might fear losing our homes or loved ones, for example, and work to do everything we can to preserve them. The fear of (physical) death is perceived as the ultimate loss.

The death of our bodies is not natural—it wasn't part of God's original plan—so our apprehension about both physical illness or demise and the loss of our earthly lives is not entirely off base. But on the level of day-to-day living, this fear is often inordinate compared to our fear of disappointing our Savior.[4] Many of us, if we're honest, fear material loss far more than we fear the spiritual loss that we may face if we do not endure to the end in our relationship with Christ. Our fear of sickness and death thus dwarfs our fear of God rather than the other way around. If we live by an eternal rather than a temporal mindset, however, we will heed Jesus' warning to his followers: "I tell you, my friends, do not fear those who kill the body, and after that have nothing more that they can do. But I will warn you whom to fear: fear him who, after he has killed, has authority to cast into hell. Yes, I tell you, fear him!" (Luke 12:4-5).

God can remedy *both* our physical and spiritual death, and thus we should fear *him*—that is, stand in holy awe of him—above all else. He must be our primary fear object.

This is a struggle when our physical ailments are acute. When we're on an operating table or dealing with chronic, daily pain, it can be hard to think of anything *but* how our bodies feel at the moment. But in those moments we may most benefit from turning our eyes upward! As C. S. Lewis put it, pain is often the megaphone that God uses to rouse a deaf world.[5]

The fact is, if we do not fear the *Lord* more than anything else, we will fear *something in the world* more than anything else. And what we fear most will reveal what we love most. Rather than fearing the loss of our material well-being more than anything, we should fear God's disappointment and displeasure above all—longing to hear his affirmative words, "Well done!" when we do finally go to be with him.

THREE WORLDS

When speaking about life and death an analogy of three worlds is helpful. The first world, which we all inhabited at one point, was womb world. None of us remembers that world, but it was designed as a *temporary* home to prepare us for the second world (the one we're in now, outside of the womb). Floating around in our mother's amniotic fluid, we had heating and air conditioning, an automatic feeding tube, and all the other provisions we needed. We could even hear the soothing voices of our parents and some other sounds, such as music, from the outside world.

Now imagine someone had communicated with you while you were still in your mother's womb. After nine months someone shouts at you, "All right, time to come out!" How many of us would have jumped at this invitation (if we could have comprehended it)? I doubt many of us would! And why would we? We have all our needs met. It's comfortable, warm, and cozy. We can hear our mother's heartbeat.

What's not to love? And yet if we stayed in womb world beyond our term, it would be a death sentence for us (and for our mother). Not only that but we'd be missing out on all that we're designed for. We would never experience the beauty of the outside world—picturesque landscapes, great music, art, fellowship, a vast array of delectable foods, and so on. We had no category for such pleasures before entering this world, though, so of course we didn't long for them in the way that we should. Nor do humans generally like change, especially a change from the familiar to the unfamiliar.

After womb world our second world is still only temporary. As wonderful as life on earth is at times, it's a precursor to a third world. Womb world was designed to prepare us for *bios* or biological life; this world is a soul-forming world that is preparing us for *zōē*, spiritual life. But here we are not in the land of the living preparing to go to the land of the dying; we are in the land of the dying preparing to go to the land of the living.

> *What we call death is actually a second birth canal.*

The third world is permanent—our final home and destiny. It's a world lived in the presence of God if we leave this second world trusting in Christ (if not, then the third world is another story entirely). Our third world is filled with eternal pleasures that our feeble imaginations can only begin to fathom now (Psalm 16:11; 1 Corinthians 13:12). The Bible offers a glimpse of that eternal home, but even then it tends to resort to metaphorical imagery to describe what heaven will be *like* (in books like Ezekiel, Daniel, and Revelation). Besides biblical prophecy, we get small hints of that third world through experiences in this world. C. S. Lewis calls them "'patches of Godlight' in the woods of our experience."[6] The reality is, we simply have no category for adequately describing or comprehending our eternal home, just as an unborn baby can't conceive of life outside the womb. For this reason even if we are cognitively sure we're on the way to a better place after we die, many of us resist the idea of leaving this world or are at least a little apprehensive about the process of getting there.

One countermeasure we can take against such resistance is to consider the greatest experiences of beauty, intimacy, and adventure we have known in this life. We can leverage them as signs of greater things since the most wonderful encounters we have had with such wonders are not what we are longing for; rather, they are *pointers* to greater goods we cannot yet name.

FOREVER YOUNG

There's a silver lining to aging, though, and it's not found in advancements in plastic surgery or the findings of modern researchers in pursuit of a medical cure for aging:

> *Age conspires with God to transfer our hope*
> *from the temporal to the eternal.*

In other words, as our bodies wear out and we begin to creak and crack and break down, we grow less and less comfortable in our earthly suits. This can make the prospect of a new body, in a new place, much more appealing. (If you're not there yet, you will be one day, Lord willing, and it will come sooner than you might think.) Of course, some people cling to their earthly bodies and fight their demise to the bitter end— going to great lengths and expense to try to defy age, cheat time, and appear forever young. But the aging process can be an important means by which God raises our sights, redirects our attachments and affections, and induces in us a more intense longing for heaven.

From the three-worlds analogy we see that God gives each of us biological life in the first two worlds; he originates life in the womb world, and then we embark on a journey of physical development (and eventual decline) from there. *Bios* is a necessary precursor to *zōē*.

Zōē (spiritual life) refers to a new quality of life that requires an initial reception—John 3:3 refers to it as the second birth—as well as ongoing growth (embracing what Paul calls the "life that is truly life" [1 Timothy 6:19 NIV]). In other words, using the terminology of the three-worlds metaphor, spiritual life begins in our second world when we first accept Jesus' offer to trust him for salvation, and it continues eternally in our third world. Galatians 2:20 describes this life this way: "I have been crucified with Christ. It is no longer I who live, but Christ who lives in me. And the life I now live in the flesh I live by faith in the Son of God, who loved me and gave himself for me" (Galatians 2:20).

The one who is born twice—first physically, second spiritually— only dies once. Our physical death is a transition, an entrance, into the world that is our final home (heaven).

The best news ever delivered to earth is that not only natural death but also spiritual death, the "last enemy" of humankind (1 Corinthians 15:26), has been defeated. Through his death and resurrection Jesus conquered death. We must keep this victory at the forefront of our minds as we grow older. This victory and the new life that accompanies it has the power to make us truly forever young—ushering in what I (Ken) like to call the second naiveté.

The first naiveté occurs when we are young and is marked by child*ish*ness. The second naiveté is a child*like*ness that constitutes an intentional curation and cultivation of growing wonder at the splendors of the world we are immersed in. Few people develop this childlike awe that keeps them supple and fresh rather than bored and rigidly inflexible. Even nonbelievers can have a kind of second naiveté, especially when interacting with nature (though they may make the mistake of directing their awe toward something or someone other than the one true Creator himself). On a spiritual level, the second naiveté comes when we become like little children when we decide to follow Jesus (Matthew 18:3). Our rebirth in

Christ ushers in a childlikeness encompassing more than wonder at the things of this world; it involves a humble attitude of submission to and awe for God in all things. This stage continues after our natural death when we enter our Father's presence and all suffering and problems are eradicated, and our deepest longings are fulfilled at last (Revelation 21:3-4).

ACCEPTANCE

Reflecting on her life at seventy-nine, Judy tells of her husband's and her recent decision to downsize their possessions:

> I have moved many times. . . . This move was different, though. All of the other moves had been associated with advancement of goals, success, acquisition. Stepping up. This one was in fact stepping down. It was associated with aging, regard for long-term finances, and a much smaller presence. We went from three beautiful homes in three states to a small high-rise condo. In the process we had to divest ourselves of many things that represented a lifetime of memories. It was not the things but the memories they represented that were hard to let go of. I also had to accept a new self-image.

Amid this significant life transition Judy finds solace in her relationship with God. "I can lose myself in time spent with Him every day," she states. She goes on to explain that, in every sense, this "new life" is better:

> As I was struggling with letting go of what I regarded as "my life," I heard Him quietly say, "Am I enough?" He did not want to hear the easy "of course" answer from my mouth. He wanted to hear a genuine "yes, of course" from my heart. In the beginning, He heard an honest, "Can I get back to you on that?" No problem saying that; He knew it already. He was going to use this very common experience as a teaching opportunity to let *me* see what

I held highest in importance. Once I found myself at peace having agreed with Him that indeed He was all I needed, He did exceedingly, abundantly more than I could have asked. . . .

Decreasing in physical and cognitive ability, worldly goods, and a circle of influence is not something to look forward to. The saving grace is seeing myself aging as a part of God's plan. As I decrease, He increases. Seeing how He steps in to fill my gaps and meet my needs makes our relationship sweeter and sweeter.

As Judy's story reveals, a healthy acceptance of the aging process (and implicitly, of our eventual physical death) can prompt righting of our course, keener attention to the direction of our bodily ship. This recognition can head off wrong prioritization as well as the presumption that we will have the time and opportunity later to get back on track if we veer off in the wrong direction. As with a ship on an ocean, even just a small move off course, which seems insignificant at first, adds up to a large difference in our final landing spot. Hence the need for God to continually reveal and hone our true perspective and practice. The earlier this happens in our lives, the better.

One of the key messages of Scripture is the need to treat the temporal as temporal and the eternal as eternal. Too often we get it backward, sometimes even unconsciously—treating the temporal as though it will last forever. If we do this, we might end up with a shiny new car or attractive physique now, but we will live with emptiness and regret later, especially if we realize we wasted much of our earlier life—the time when we had the most physical vitality—on things that won't matter in the end. Jesus warned us of this temptation in the parable of the rich fool.

He told them a parable, saying, "The land of a rich man produced plentifully, and he thought to himself, 'What shall I do, for I have nowhere to store my crops?' And he said, 'I will do this: I will tear down my barns and build larger ones, and there I will store all my grain and my goods. And I will say to my soul, "Soul, you have ample goods laid up for many years; relax, eat, drink, be merry." But God said to him, 'Fool! This night your soul is required of you, and the things you have prepared, whose will they be?' So is the one who lays up treasure for himself and is not rich toward God." (Luke 12:16-21)

The book of James offers a similar warning:

Come now, you who say, "Today or tomorrow we will go into such and such a town and spend a year there and trade and make a profit"—yet you do not know what tomorrow will bring. What is your life? For you are a mist that appears for a little time and then vanishes. Instead you ought to say, "If the Lord wills, we will live and do this or that." As it is, you boast in your arrogance. All such boasting is evil. (James 4:13-16)

Recognizing our mortality—numbering our days or seeing our lives as a vanishing mist—is an important step toward an attitude of humility before God rather than arrogance. Humility acknowledges that our time—the exact number of days, hours, and minutes he has appointed for us to be alive on earth—is in his hands (Job 14:5-6). This change in attitude in turn results in correct priorities, as we come to treasure that which endures over that which is passing away.

There's a delicate balance to achieve here. We are not advocating dualism—that worldview that sees everything material as evil. To be sure, our physical bodies are "instruments for righteousness," temples of the Holy Spirit, to be used in service to him (Romans 6:13). Matter is not bad, and we are to care for (steward) all that God entrusts us with. At the same time we should not obsess over or idolize the exteriors of our lives, "polishing brass on a sinking ship," as the saying goes. This is easier said than done, as our hearts are being wrenched away from the things most of us cling to from the time we're young. But it must be done and, again, the earlier the better.

Recalibrating

My (Jenny's) father is in his sixties and has struggled with heart disease and declining physical energy for over a decade now. His experiences have given me personal insight into the ups and downs of aging, including the alternating cycles of discouragement and encouragement that can accompany it. This process is hard to watch as a child, and it makes me cognizant of my tendencies to try to ignore or downplay the realities of aging and death. My father writes, "Every day I feel I am being separated from this world and all of its temporary consolations and tribulations, driven toward the next world and its eternal securities. . . . Heaven is the goal, though I am not ready to go there yet, and I am no longer at home on this earth either!" His sentiment is reminiscent of Paul's, described in his letter to the Philippians written from prison: "For to me to live is Christ, and to die is gain. . . . I am hard pressed between the two. My desire is to depart and be with Christ, for that is far better" (Philippians 1:21, 23).

As the end of our lives approaches and our difficulties grow, many of us feel a similar tension. This tension is not only okay but even biblical, for we really are straddling two worlds. Eternal life (defined in Scripture as *knowing Christ* [John 17:3]) has begun, and yet we remain in this time-trapped world for a bit longer.

> *Ideally, we won't wait until our forties or later to learn the wisdom of living with an awareness of how fleeting life is. The beauty of godly wisdom is that it's available to anyone of any age.*

Regardless of our age, when we truly grasp and accept the fact that our lives on earth don't go on forever, and we stop putting off thoughts about the inevitable, we will be able to see more clearly the (spiritual) reality that supersedes (indeed, supplants) the visible reality we see each day. At that point God can move us from fear to faith, from the illusions of autonomy and control that the world invites us to pursue to a deep hope in the One who is bringing all things to a triumphant, victorious end—which is not an end at all but the continuation of the journey that began in this life.

We're all citizens of another country, a place we were designed for, where we will at last find our true sense of belonging and where "death shall be no more" (Revelation 21:4). We may not always like the process it takes to get to that place, but we can approach it without the pit of dread that fills someone who does not have Christ. Because if we have Christ, we truly have everything—all that we need in this life, and a glorious future to anticipate in the life to come.

· · · · · · · · · · · · · · ·
READ AND REFLECT ON
Psalm 90
· · · · · · · · · · · · · · ·

Consider memorizing verses 12, 14

Prayer: Lord, may I be assured of the new life I have in you. May I not be consumed with fear of death or dying. I want to gain a heart of wisdom. Therefore, please help me number my days—that is, long for and live each day in light of *that* Day when I will see you face-to-face and live forever in your presence. Help me to do this every day, not only today. Amen.

CHAPTER THREE

TREASURING GOD AND PEOPLE

In this is love, not that we have loved God but that he loved us
and sent his Son to be the propitiation for our sins. Beloved,
if God so loved us, we also ought to love one another.

1 JOHN 4:10-11

There's a classic scene in the 1991 movie *City Slickers* where a father, Mitch (played by Billy Crystal), speaks to his son's elementary school class. After introducing himself and explaining what he does for his job, he delivers this motivational speech:

> Value this time in your life, kids, because this is the time in your life when you still have your choices. It goes by so fast. When you're a teenager, you think you can do anything, and you do. Your twenties are a blur. Your thirties, you raise your family, you make some money, you think to yourself, "What happened to my twenties?" Your forties, you grow a little pot belly, you grow another chin, the music starts to get too loud, one of your old

girlfriends from high school becomes a grandmother. In your fifties, you have a minor surgery—you'll call it a "procedure," but it's a surgery. In your sixties, you'll have a major surgery, the music is still loud, but it doesn't matter, because you can't hear it anyway. The seventies, you and the wife retire to Fort Lauderdale, you start eating dinner at two o'clock in the afternoon, you have lunch around ten, breakfast the night before, and you spend most of your time wandering around malls looking for the ultimate soft yogurt and muttering, "How come the kids don't call? How come the kids don't call?" In the eighties, you'll have a major stroke; you end up babbling to some Jamaican nurse who your wife can't stand, but who you call mama. Any questions?[1]

The youngsters' eyes grow wider, their jaws dropping, as Mitch drones on about his depressing outlook on life. The message is clear: *It's all downhill from here, kids.*

Encouragingly, in the movie Mitch—in the throes of a somewhat stereotypical midlife crisis—embarks on a mission to recapture a sense of meaning in his life by visiting a dude ranch with friends. During a cattle drive with friends, he meets an older cowboy named Curly. Here's a slice of their famous "one thing" dialogue:

CURLY	You know what the secret of life is?
MITCH	No, what?
CURLY	(holding up his leather-gloved hand and pointing with his index finger) This.
MITCH	Your finger?
CURLY	One thing, just one thing.
MITCH	That's great, but what's the one thing?
CURLY	That's what you've got to figure out.

In the end Mitch discovers that the secret of life isn't a formula; rather, the "one thing" central to living a meaningful life is relationships.

There's truth in Mitch's discovery, but by itself it carries us only so far. The movie offers little clue about the ultimate purpose of relationships (including their divine origin) and how to make them succeed on a practical level. Mitch rightly recognizes the fact that people matter more than success and wealth and other worldly pursuits, but when the curtain is drawn, he's missing the spiritual foundation and the practical principles needed to empower the one thing that makes our lives count.

Because of their centrality to life, relationships are central to the recalibration process. Without an eternal perspective on people (viewing them as God views them), it will be impossible to recalibrate well. In addition, other people are often the very tool God uses to help us recalibrate.

OUR ONE THING

Jesus was once asked a question similar to the one Mitch was asking (What's the secret of life?). A lawyer among the Pharisees, putting Jesus to the test, asked, "Teacher, which is the great commandment in the Law?" (Matthew 22:36). In the Jewish world he might as well have been asking, "Of all the things God has laid out in his law, what's the secret—the most important thing—in life?" Jesus lands in the same place Mitch landed on a surface level: life is all about relationships. But Jesus' reply takes us where a Hollywood movie won't:

> [Jesus] said to him, "'You shall love the Lord your God with all your heart and with all your soul and with all your mind.' This is the great and first commandment. And the second is like it, 'You shall love your neighbor as yourself.' On these two commandments depend all the Law and the Prophets." (Matthew 22:37-40)

Jesus is emphasizing that the most important priority in life, regardless of life stage or situation, is indeed *relationships*. Every other command ultimately falls under this larger umbrella. But notice the order of Jesus' words in particular: a life well-lived focuses, *first*, on a right relationship with God and, *second*, on relationships with our fellow humans. (There's also an implied third relationship in the mix— our relationship with ourselves since we are to love others *as* ourselves.) In other words the secret to life is prioritizing our vertical relationship with God—loving him with all our being—and then allowing that relationship to animate and empower our relationships on the horizontal plane (with other people and ourselves). Without this correct ordering, our relationships will fail, both in practice and in purpose, affecting our entire lives.

> *Only by drawing on God's power and resources will the rest of our relationships live up to their potential and have the eternal impact he intends.*

In *Conformed to His Image*, I (Ken) speak of this key to life as "loving God completely." Loving God, in turn, fuels our ability to "love ourselves correctly" (defined as seeing ourselves as God sees us) and "love others compassionately." To summarize, "because the infinite and personal God loves us, he wants us to grow in an intimate relationship with him; this is the purpose for which we were created—to know, love, enjoy, and honor the triune Lord of all creation."[2] Because God is a relational being, the two Great Commandments of loving him and expressing this love for him by loving others are also intensely relational. We were created for fellowship and intimacy not only with God but also with each other.

Thus, the ultimate goal of relationships goes far beyond the world's concept; for the follower of Christ they are a primary way we manifest our love for God. In fact, the Bible goes so far as to say that our love for others is evidence of our love for God—if we say we love God but hate other people, we are liars (1 John 4:20). The basis of this idea is the unique recognition in Christianity of the infinite worth of all people, a worth demonstrated by the fact that Christ gave up his life to save ours. Human worth is ultimately rooted in the reality that humankind bears the image of God (Genesis 1:26-27). Whether individuals acknowledge this image-bearing reality is not the issue. The Bible says, like it or not, all human beings are created in God's image.

Therefore, we are to love others not because we deem them worth loving or because they are followers of God like us or even because they share DNA with us; we love them as an extension of our love for God, who made them (as he made us) in his image. (By the way, even many atheists admit in their actions if not their words to the intrinsic value of human life; in loving their family members and others, they actually live better than their worldview dictates.)

DEFINING LOVE

Relationships are the currency of heaven, then, and our love for others evidences our love for God. But before we delve into what makes relationships work on a practical level, we need to understand what it means to see and love people as God wants us to see and love them.

Besides the tremendous confusion today about human sexual love (*eros*) and romantic relationships (a confusion that isn't new—just resurrected in new ways), there is a common temptation in every age to view people and relationships in a utilitarian manner. We love and give and serve because others have done the same for us or because we expect them to do so in the future. In other words the fleshly instinct is to view and use people for our selfish purposes, sometimes even unconsciously, whether it's to feel better about ourselves, to gain a sense of personal significance or worth, or to further ourselves somehow. We even do this with our family members, including children!

Borrowing loosely from Augustine, we can define love as *the steady intention of the will toward another's highest good.* This definition emphasizes the biblical idea that love is not a feeling but a choice, an act of the will. Aiming for others' highest good takes us away from a people-pleasing approach and a permissive approach that offers approval of behavior without regard for God's standards, focusing instead on that which is truly good for a person, from God's viewpoint. In a broad sense the highest good, of course, is that a person may know and love God.

Far from permitting us to take an excessively tough or harsh approach toward others (especially when their sin becomes evident to us), this definition challenges us to model the character of Christ in how we love others—with compassion, patience, kindness, selflessness, and all the other traits found in 1 Corinthians 13:4-7. This love isn't flabby, nor is it cheap: "God demonstrates His own love toward us, in that while we were yet sinners, Christ died for us" (Romans 5:8 NASB).

God's love for us is causeless and undeserved. His love led him to give up his most prized possession, his Son. "God's love is manifested in the fact that he is a giver. From the beginning, he has given even though people have rejected his gifts more than received them."[3] Likewise, our relationships with people are to be fueled by the love, grace, and kindness our Creator has shown us, not by what they have done for us or by what they can or will do for us. This runs counter to our fleshly instinct!

LOVE IN ACTION

Myriad Scriptures emphasize the causeless nature of God's love. Let's look at one snapshot in the life of Jesus to understand better how this divine love is applied to day-to-day relationships.

In Mark 5:21-43 Jesus is surrounded by crowds, as was typical. Suddenly, one of the most important religious rulers in town, Jairus, comes to him and throws himself at Jesus' feet, begging him to heal his sick daughter. Jairus has done nothing for Jesus (that we know of), and yet Jesus drops everything to help him.

As Jesus goes, however, he welcomes a second interruption. This time it's not an influential man but a marginalized woman (remember, in that society women did not hold the status they do today). This woman had been sick with a bleeding affliction for twelve years, and because of her uncleanness she would not have been allowed to enter the synagogue that entire time. This woman had no positive marks in the religious-piety column; because of her social status (an outcast) she would likely never be able to do anything to thank Jesus if he were to help her. And yet again Jesus ignores the pressures from the crowds, stops everything to heal her when she touches his robe, and speaks tenderly to her, "Daughter, your faith has made you well; go in peace, and be healed of your disease" (v. 34).

Jesus' delay seems to have irritated at least some members of Jairus's household who thought Jesus was now too late to help them and thus shouldn't be bothered anymore (v. 35). But the Lord continues with his mission and goes on to do another miracle—raising the elite man's daughter from the dead.

Jesus' willingness to halt his activities to help individuals one on one, people who had done nothing for him or could do nothing in return, is instructive. The Son of God could have been the busiest man on this earth, unwilling to be bothered with a father's concern for his daughter or with a poor woman's malady. But Jesus never saw himself as too important to serve anyone God put in his path. God his Father and the people he came to save were his chief priorities (in that order), and nothing could derail him from that focus.

We too are called to set aside our agendas and embrace the unexpected moments and interruptions in our day-to-day living, seeing every relational encounter as an opportunity to show another person the love of God. True love for others isn't a matter of talk. It is acted on in deeds of service that consider others' needs above our own. While this attitude may go unnoticed by the world, it is greatness in the kingdom of God. Francis Schaeffer wrote that "there are no little people" in God's kingdom; likewise, there are no little (or inconsequential) acts of love if they are done with the right attitude (Matthew 25:40).[4] For this reason we must never measure the value of our lives by the world's standards but by love—the love God has shown us through his Son, and the love he pours in and through us to others (1 John 4:10-11).

RELATIONSHIPS WITHOUT REGRET

If you talk to people approaching the end of their lives (or those who interact often with such people, like hospice and palliative care workers), it is almost without exception that some people's primary end-of-life regrets are in the area of relationships. A high percentage wish they had

+ spent less time working and more time with family, especially their kids when they were young

+ done more for other people

+ been a better spouse or parent

When we recalibrate, we do well to pay close attention to the relationships in our lives so we will avoid such regrets.

If people and relationships are so important, why do we fail in them so often? Of course, there are myriad reasons, many of them rooted in human sinfulness (e.g., pride, fear, selfishness).

When sin first entered the world, remember that Adam and Eve covered themselves—they hid both from God (the relationship of primary importance in their lives) and each other (as shame and blame took over, breaking their communion as a couple). So human failure in relationships dates to the fall. Yet in Christ we find the power for success in this area—an ability to enjoy genuine community where there was once alienation, to love (friend and foe alike) instead of hate. With our security in him we find the courage to reconcile with others, even if it means admitting our wrongdoing or risking being hurt or persecuted or slandered. With our identity in him and not in our per-formance or possessions, we find the motivation to place eternal souls above other, temporal priorities.

Besides human sinfulness, many of us fail in relationships simply out of neglect—we don't work on them. We may conveniently focus on those who are easy to love while ignoring people we don't like very much or with whom our relationships never seem to improve. Yet even the best of relationships hit rough spots and can take a downward turn.

The second law of thermodynamics comes in handy here. This law is about degeneration and decay. Essentially, it says that the quantity of useful energy in a closed system gradually diminishes over time. This principle can apply not only to thermodynamic systems but to other systems, including the web of human relationships. The bottom line is this:

Relationships left to themselves atrophy.

They fall into disorder and diminish in quality without a steady in-fusion of intentional energy. We see this in marriages often. Romantic or erotic love simply can't sustain a marriage over the long term; even friendship has its limits in marriage because humans are inherently sinful and selfish. As time goes by, without an intentional choice to be other-centered, a man and a woman eventually descend into a self-centered, broken (or breaking) relationship. They may still choose to live under the same roof (often for pragmatic reasons), but the initial sense of intimacy fades and they become near-strangers to each other.

All relationships face similar dangers and, like marriage, take effort. We cannot take a passive approach, because relationships simply will not sustain and grow themselves. Many of us are experts at postponing the effort we need to put forth in our relationships. We are *all* guilty of this to some degree if we're honest. We presume upon the future. We prioritize the urgent—the project at the office, the chores around the house, and other obligations. In the process we defer our care and love for the *people* right in front of us until a later date. But what if that date never comes? There will *always* be something urgent competing for our attention!

Personal technology has made this natural tendency worse. We can live in the same household, be in the same room as another person, and if we're too immersed in our phones or other devices, almost imperceptibly over time we slowly lose touch with the people around us: with others, with God, even with ourselves. It is too easy to start to believe the lie that a small rectangular device is all we need—that what is happening in the world of our devices is more urgent and more important than what is happening in the tactile world around us. Nearly all of us who use a device connected to the internet fall into this temptation. And we all must continually guard against it. There can be nothing worse than getting to the end of our lives and realizing we spent years of our lives staring at a screen—yes, sometimes toward good ends, but more often than we'd like to admit toward wasted and futile ends. Phones are a helpful tool for some aspects of relationships, but they are poor masters and are no substitute for real presence and fellowship.

LOVING UNTIL THE END

> *If we're to live a meaningful life, and if we're to transition well from stage to stage, relationships must take a front seat in all we do.*

If our plans and goals center on ourselves—on grabbing instead of giving, on finding comfort and pleasure for ourselves rather than showing compassion to others—then we've missed the heart of the Christian life. This doesn't mean we ignore our own needs at the expense of others (we're to love others *as we love ourselves*, Jesus reinforced), but neither should we become so focused on ourselves that we neglect those around us.

Prioritizing people will look different in everyone's life. God is not concerned with appearances or quantity; he looks at our hearts. Serving others quietly without anyone's knowledge—whether it's the postal worker we see daily or the nurse at our bedside or the child or parent we are taking care of—is just as laudable as loving and serving in more visible ways. Participating in and serving a local community of believers can be just as God-honoring if all we do is serve as a greeter at the door or volunteer in the nursery; we need not be a pastor or a more prominent person in our church to be a spiritual leader. The most admired heroes of the faith, the greatest champions of God's love and work in the world, do not trumpet their good deeds or do them for the recognition of others. We're called to live for an audience of One.

Corrie ten Boom, best known for her heroism and survival during the Holocaust, lived her entire life with a laser focus on serving God by serving other people. Most don't know much about either her early years or her last years of life, but they're just as remarkable as the period so well documented in *The Hiding Place*. Described in a biography fitly named *The Five Silent Years of Corrie ten Boom* (written by her caregiver Pamela Rosewell), ten Boom's final days on earth were marked by the same love, service, and prayer-centeredness that had characterized her for decades. Even when a stroke in her eighties rendered her bedridden and mute, she found ways of serving and loving God and others.

> There had been a tremendous change in her way of life, one that could crush her spirit—but that had not happened. . . . I could see no difference in the attitude of this weak and silent Tante Corrie to that of the strong speaker whom I had joined nearly three years earlier. She served Him then; she was serving Him now. . . . She had served Him in her youth; now she was serving Him in her old age. . . . [God's view] of her had not changed although in the eyes of an achievement-oriented society she may have lost her usefulness. . . .

Each day when she was well enough, she received visitors. Many of them remarked to us about the peaceful atmosphere of [her house], and referred to Tante Corrie's undiminished spiritual gift of discernment. "Those eyes of hers . . . they looked right inside me."

Her lips could no longer say, "Jesus is Victor," but her life could, and it did. . . . She still had a great love for people, and God enabled her to communicate that love without words.[5]

Rosewell goes on to describe several examples of this inaudible communication that took place between ten Boom and the visitors at her bedside—some of them strangers. These ranged from a police officer patrolling the neighborhood to a flower shop delivery lady (who had delivered flowers to ten Boom a year earlier but came back after never being able to forget the "life and love in Tante Corrie's eyes") to a teenager named Bob, who stated, "When I met her, such a love came from her that I immediately stopped the wrong things I was getting into."[6]

Make no mistake, ten Boom's relational impact had nothing to do with her fame (though that fame may have brought people to her that otherwise would never have met her). Rather, it came from a life surrendered to God, in which her daily question was how she could love the next person she saw.

RECALIBRATING

Two things on earth endure in the end, people and God's Word. Our time on earth is best spent investing the latter into the former. Corrie ten Boom modeled this perfectly, and her story offers powerful encouragement to those weakened by health troubles or simply worn out from life. Even in her declining health, the radiance of Christ shone unmistakably in her. Fully accepting of her condition, never rebellious toward God, and yet aware that as long as she had life and breath God still had a purpose for her on earth, she used what few capacities she still had to love people. Her example is also instructive to those of us who are younger, for her legacy and impact were the product of a *lifelong*, ever-growing faith.

Ten Boom had the words "My times are in Your hands" posted on her wall (taken from Psalm 31:15). Her life is proof positive that God is not limited by our limitations. In fact, he often works most mightily in and through our weaknesses (2 Corinthians 12:9-10).

When ten Boom found herself in a Nazi concentration camp in midlife, she frequently risked her safety to tell others about Christ, never knowing if she had another day to live. (Her sister, Betsie, who entered the concentration camp with Corrie, did not make it out.) For all of us it is wise to live each day as though it were our last and to treat each person as though we may never see them again. Living well and without regrets means

✦ not leaving unfinished business in relationships

✦ not deferring our love to another day (when it's more convenient or we are less busy)

✦ speaking our love, gratitude, and forgiveness *today*—or at the earliest opportunity we get (see Matthew 5:23-25; Proverbs 3:27)

We encourage you to take time for tool 6, designed to help you assess and recalibrate the relational aspect of your life. Don't miss the part about looking for people to invest in and at least one person to mentor you. Humbly walking under the mentorship of believers who are wiser (and often, though not always, older) can be one of the most beneficial things you will do.

READ AND REFLECT ON
1 John 4:7-11

Prayer: Lord, may I always place a high priority on the people you have sovereignly placed in my life. May you love them through me, and may I never stop looking for ways to love, pray for, and serve others, even when it may be difficult or inconvenient for me. Amen.

TOOL 6: RELATIONSHIP ASSESSMENT

The Great Commandments indicate that life is all about relationships—our relationship with God first, from whom flows the power to establish successful relationships with other people. Without the love of God pouring into us first, we will not be able to love our neighbors as ourselves.

Following is an assessment to help you gain a picture of how well you are treasuring the relationships in your life—the vertical one (with God) and the horizontal ones (with other people). Although some of us are naturally more relational than others, we are all called to love others with whom we come in contact.

Relationship with God

✦ Do you spend time with God? How often?

✦ What is your time with him like? How's your communication? Is it one-sided or do you take time to both talk and listen to him in prayer?

✦ What's one thing you can do to spur growth in your relationship with God?

Relationships with People

Think about your

✦ nuclear family members (spouse and kids, if married; parents, if they are alive; other close relatives)

✦ close friends who are believers

✦ close friends who are nonbelievers

✦ work colleagues (coworkers and boss)

Honestly assess each of these four categories and list the relationships (names) that are

✦ strong and growing

✦ weak or difficult

✦ stagnant/in danger of atrophying

Various Scriptures advise us not to leave unfinished business in our relationships—at the end of our lives *or* at the end of a day (after all, none of us can guarantee tomorrow). To that end,

✦ Confess bitterness and unforgiveness in any relationships in your life.

✦ Act on God's command to make things right (if you are able) as quickly as possible.

Mentoring and accountability should be a part of every growing believer's life. Consider,

✦ Who is investing in *you* right now (as a coach or mentor—either formally or informally)?

✦ If nobody, do you desire to look for someone to mentor or counsel/disciple you? Is there a likely candidate, someone who is already positioned to take this role in your life? (Keep in mind, although the dynamic will not be the same, we can also be mentored by deceased people—authors, preachers, teachers, and other servants of God who speak to us through their writings or recorded sermons.)

✦ Who are you investing in right now, in some sort of mentoring type of relationship?

✦ If nobody, is there someone you could seek out—a younger person who might benefit from your interest, care, and counsel? Commit to contacting them to see if they would like to meet with you to explore the possibility of a regular meeting time.

God's Word and People

People (immortal beings) and the Word of God are the two things from this earth that go on for eternity; thus, the most powerful and lasting investment we can make is to invest the latter into the former.

✦ How are you investing God's Word into other people?

✦ Prayerfully consider if there is something more God is leading you to do on this front.

Note: You may want to revisit this tool after reading chapter fourteen, which discusses specific ideas about how to wisely steward our relationships on earth.

CHAPTER FOUR

MOVING FROM CAREER TO CALLING

Whatever you do, work heartily,
as for the Lord and not for men.

COLOSSIANS 3:23

A decade of indulging his darkest vices" is how once–nightclub promoter Scott Harrison described his career prior to declaring "spiritual, moral, and emotional bankruptcy." A timely encounter with an influential book and a two-year stint on a ship off the coast of Liberia changed everything.[1]

In 2006 Harrison founded Charity: Water, a nonprofit dedicated to "bring[ing] clean water to every person living without it."[2] In fourteen years the organization raised more than a half-billion dollars and funded more than 78,000 water projects that will bring clean, safe drinking water to over thirteen million people. Harrison's work today contrasts starkly with the first part of his career: "At twenty-eight years old, Scott Harrison had it all. A top nightclub promoter in New York City, his life was an endless cycle of drugs, booze, and parties."[3] And it all unraveled.

I was the worst person I knew. I'd walked away from all the spirituality and morality I'd embraced as a child, and felt completely bankrupt. I got people wasted for a living in nightclubs, and effectively the drunker they got, the more money I made. I started reading a book by A. W. Tozer called *The Pursuit of God*, and it just really rocked me. Here was an author trying to serve God desperately, living a life of submission and a life of service, and my life looked exactly opposite. Everything was about me.[4]

Early one morning, sitting in a nightclub, Harrison gave his life to the One he'd come to New York to escape. Feeling like the prodigal son, he left his life in the city and volunteered as a photojournalist for Mercy Ships, a ministry that sends floating hospitals to provide hope and healing around the world.[5] Off the coast of Liberia his entrepreneurial spirit was reignited—this time leading him to an idea that would *help* rather than *destroy* lives.[6] The vision for Charity: Water was born. Though not a religious organization the nonprofit uses a unique donor model to meet a basic human need. Through this, Harrison and his colleagues recognize the dignity, love, and provision God desires to pour out on those who bear his image.

Harrison's story illustrates the dramatic difference our work can make both in our lives and the lives of others, either for better or for worse. It also highlights the inescapable reality that our work is an expression of our faith and identity—who we are, what we believe about God, and what we believe about other human beings as well as the world we inhabit.

Transitions and Pitfalls

As adults we spend the vast majority of our waking hours working. Because of the dominant place work has in our lives, if only in terms of the sheer number of hours spent, we must develop an eternal perspective on this sphere of life. Such a perspective will give us a framework for operating on a daily basis and a reference point for recalibrating.

The work sphere of life (along with relationships) is one in which we experience some of our most tumultuous life transitions—changes that we choose and changes forced on us against our will:

✦ launching a career for the first time (after high school, college, or graduate school)

✦ switching careers

✦ launching an entrepreneurial endeavor

✦ losing a job or facing unemployment

✦ being promoted (leading to more responsibility)

✦ becoming a stay-at-home parent

✦ retiring

✦ job hunting later in life (e.g., as an empty nester or a retiree needing some supplemental income)

Without a biblical worldview underpinning all we do in the area of work, we will be prone to a host of common pitfalls, leading to a personal crisis, regret, or even harm to ourselves or others:

✦ overworking (often to the neglect of ourselves or our family and other relationships)

✦ being unwilling to work and thus becoming a burden or even disruptive to others (2 Thessalonians 3:11)

✦ finding our identity, security, and significance in our work more than in Christ (leading to idolatry and eventually discontentment, disillusionment, and dissatisfaction)

✦ seeing our work solely as the means to a paycheck (which may lead us to toil at a job for years without regard to our unique, God-given skills and aspirations)

✦ being driven instead of called (often leading to frustration and overwork rather than joy and fulfillment)[7]

Whether early or late in life, we can always make midcourse adjustments in the area of work. Scott Harrison did so while still in his twenties, but others have done so much later in life—some by choice, some out of necessity. Our goal should be to continually seek to align our perspective and practice in the sphere of work (just as in other areas of life) to God's rather than conform to the surrounding culture.

It's important to make a distinction here: the work we do for a job or career (or even as a full-time homemaker or parent) is not the same as our vocation. *Vocation* comes from the Latin word *vocare*, meaning "to call." Our calling from God is lifelong; it transcends our roles and seasons of life. We never retire from our vocation. Ideally, our work (career and other types of work) is *one* outworking of our unique purpose or calling (this was certainly the case for Scott Harrison). But this isn't always true. For example, the apostle Paul's vocation or calling was to preach the gospel as the apostle to the Gentiles, but his trade was tentmaking. That work provided income to fund his ministry travel and basic needs, thus helping him avoid becoming a burden on churches that might feel obliged to support him. Ken's friend Neal was a general contractor in home construction before he retired and became a part-time contracting consultant to support his Christian leadership ministry.

We will speak to the larger topic of purpose or calling in part two. This chapter focuses on helping you to see (or resee) your work as a means to a higher end instead of something to just get through or earn a paycheck. To gain this eternal perspective on work, we need to answer a few important questions:

1. Why do we work?

2. Who do we work for?

3. Does the type of work we do matter to God?

4. Does our work endure? (If so, how?)

Why Do We Work and Who Do We Work For?

Work is (or at least *should be*) for more than money, and it's done primarily for God, not our employer or ourselves.

Work was created by God *before* the fall, not as a result of it.[8] Work is, in fact, a part of the created order for humanity that God declared "good" (Genesis 1:28, 31; 2:5, 15) and is patterned after the Creator himself (Exodus 20:11). God's work of creating the heavens and the earth is why we who bear his image are also called to *work*, to *create*.

Let us clarify here that *work* as a term can refer to a variety of activities, from paid employment to volunteer work to domestic work (as in childrearing, cooking, gardening, etc.) to work directly for God's kingdom (i.e., missions and ministry [cf. 2 Timothy 2:15]). Besides reflecting our Creator's character, all of these kinds of work, according to the Bible, have the following benefits:

- ✦ It is an admirable and satisfying way of life, giving us independence so we are not a drain on other people (1 Thessalonians 4:11).
- ✦ It keeps us from being lazy or idle—and ultimately from becoming a burden to others or from living a life of poverty or even destruction (2 Thessalonians 3:8, 11-12; Proverbs 10:4; 16:9; 21:25).
- ✦ It is one (though not the only) means God uses to meet our temporal needs (2 Thessalonians 3:10).
- ✦ It is one context in which we can love, serve, bless, and meet the needs of others.
- ✦ It can give us possessions, wealth, and positions that we can leverage for kingdom purposes.

In all of these benefits it's important to remember that *God* is ultimately our provider; he is the one who gives us the opportunity, privilege, and ability to work (Deuteronomy 8:18). We do not meet our own needs, but he does, and he often does so through our work. He also helps meet others' needs through our work (see, for example, his instruction to the Israelites to leave the gleaning of a harvest for the "poor and the sojourner" [Leviticus 23:22]).

Unfortunately, because of the fall, work is now associated with toil more than joy (Genesis 3:17-19). A lush land, once easy and rewarding to tend, became filled with "thorns and thistles" (Genesis 3:18), making work, well, *difficult*. Besides affecting the relative difficulty of work, the fall also means that the realm of work is pervaded by sin— our own and others'. Work can be driven by wrong motivations, such as greed, vanity, and pride. It can become a means of exploitation and oppression as it did in the case of the Egyptians.

> So [the Egyptians] appointed taskmasters over [the Israelites] to afflict them with hard labor. And they built for Pharaoh storage cities, Pithom and Raamses. But the more they afflicted them, the more they multiplied and the more they spread out, so that they were in dread of the sons of Israel. The Egyptians compelled the sons of Israel to labor rigorously; and they made their lives bitter with hard labor in mortar and bricks and at all *kinds* of labor in the field, all their labors which they rigorously imposed on them. (Exodus 1:11-14 NASB)

Thankfully, work, like other spheres of life, is filled with redemptive possibilities for followers of Jesus.

Our toil, though still touched by the fall to an extent, can be infused with purpose when we approach it with an eternal perspective— and when we realize we're ultimately working for God.

Two verses in Colossians sum up the attitude of stewardship, service, and worship that we are to have in approaching our work, as well as *any* activity:

> Whatever you do in word or deed, *do* all in the name of the Lord Jesus, giving thanks through Him to God the Father. (Colossians 3:17 NASB)

Whatever you do, do your work heartily, as for the Lord rather than for men. (Colossians 3:23 NASB)

In other words our work serves many purposes, but chief among them is the eternal purpose of pleasing and serving our heavenly Father. This truth was not lost on composer Johann Sebastian Bach. He famously signed much of his music "S. D. G." The initials stand for *Soli Deo gloria* (meaning, "to God, alone, the glory"), representing the fact that he saw his work (creating music) first and foremost as an offering to God.

INTEGRATING WORK WITH LIFE

The way Bach saw his work reflects the holistic mindset all believers should have toward their work and activities: the Christian life is integrated. It isn't divided into a dichotomy of the sacred and the secular. Rather, everything we do can be infused with meaning when we work for God in the power that he supplies us. Who we are and what we do on the clock should be related to and in harmony with who we are and what we do off the clock (in the evenings, on the weekends, and during vacations and holidays). *All* we do (unless, of course, it's blatantly sinful—as Scott Harrison's work was before he came to faith) can be done in the presence and for the glory of God.[9]

Writing in the twentieth century, Dorothy Sayers advocated this integrated view of work in her essay (first presented in a speech in 1942), titled "Why Work?":

> [The Church] has allowed work and religion to become separate departments, and is astonished to find that, as a result, the secular work of the world is turned to purely selfish and destructive ends. . . .
>
> But is it astonishing? How can one remain interested in a religion which seems to have no concern with nine-tenths of his life? The Church's approach to an intelligent carpenter is usually confined to exhorting him not to be drunk and disorderly in his leisure

hours, and to come to church on Sundays. What the Church should be telling him is this: that the very first demand that his religion makes upon him is that he should make good tables.

Church by all means, and decent forms of amusement, certainly—but what use is all that if in the very center of his life and occupation he is insulting God with bad carpentry? No crooked table legs or ill-fitting drawers ever, I dare swear, came out of the carpenter's shop at Nazareth. Nor, if they did, could anyone believe that they were made by the same hand that made Heaven and earth.[10]

Echoing Sayers's sentiment, modern-day author and minister Skye Jethani traces the roots of the sacred-secular divide that we so often see in the church's attitude toward work:

The idea dates back to Eusebius, the bishop of Caesarea in the fourth century . . . [who] wrote that Christ had established two ways of life, the "perfect life" and the "permitted life." The perfect life was the one God called the clergy to—a life of prayer, worship, and service to Christ through the church. Other occupations, while necessary, carried less dignity. The labor of farmers, artists, merchants, and homemakers was not evil, but neither was it blessed, nor were these roles callings from God. . . .

This hierarchy of labor went largely unchallenged until the Protestant Reformation. Leaders like Martin Luther and John Calvin called Christians back to the authority of Scripture, and there they found no justification for the exaltation of the clergy or the abasement of other labor. . . .

Luther wrote, "The works of monks and priests, however holy and arduous they be, do not differ one whit in the sight of God from the works of the rustic laborer in the field or the woman going about her household tasks, but that all works are measured before God by faith alone."

With this recalibration of the doctrine of vocation, many came to view their labor differently, not as menial labor to be endured but as a God-ordained calling to be pursued with religious zeal. It resulted in a new devotion to work that historians refer to as "the Protestant work ethic," and it was coupled with a vision that Christ was actively engaged in every part of the world—not just the church.[11]

Today, most believers understand in theory—though we don't always demonstrate in practice—that whether we're a musician, carpenter, nurse, teacher, accountant, homemaker, or some other type of worker, as long as we're in an honest profession (not a blatantly sinful one), we can ultimately work *for* God and his glory. Our workplace (whether a home, office, studio, classroom, or hospital) becomes a sanctuary or cathedral— the setting and context in which we serve him as an act of worship.[12]

DOES THE TYPE OF WORK WE DO MATTER?

Martin Luther King Jr. famously preached:

If it falls to one's lot to be a street sweeper, he should at that moment seek to sweep streets like Michelangelo carved marble, like Rafael painted pictures. He should seek to sweep streets like Beethoven composed the music or like Shakespeare wrote poetry. He should seek to sweep streets so well that all the hosts of heaven and earth will have to pause and say, "Here lived a great street sweeper, and he swept his job well."[13]

King's words raise the question, Does the *type* of job we do matter? If God can be glorified no matter what we do, does he care if we choose to become a street sweeper instead of an engineer, a teacher instead of a lawyer, or a pediatrician instead of an elementary school teacher?

Although having a heart focused on honoring God certainly matters *most* in our work, this doesn't mean every profession is an equivalent path for us personally. God made each one of us individually, with a unique combination of skills, spiritual gifts, life experiences, personality traits, and position both on the globe and in history. We benefit from becoming aware of how God made us, including both our strengths and weaknesses.

So, how *do* we choose our work? And how do we know if it's time to make a change in this area—to recalibrate?

Some of that answer will come in part two when we discuss purpose, but here we can say a few things pertaining directly to a career.

COMBINING SKILL AND PASSION

Many people make the mistake of choosing a profession exclusively (or almost exclusively) based on salary: *What will pay the bills or lead to the level of income I wish to have?* Although finances are a legitimate factor in choosing our work, our job shouldn't *merely* be about earning a paycheck (or any other earthly reward—such as others' approval and recognition). We will eventually burn out from work that draws income but fails to capture or exercise our gifts. We will tend to develop a love-hate relationship with that work, enjoying the benefits of the job and feeling the need to continue slaving away, but deep down wishing we could abandon it and spend time doing what we *really* want to do. This attitude often leads us to live more in the future than in the present, and it may cause us to miss opportunities God is putting right in front of us.

It helps to evaluate our work in light of three factors:

1. passion (what you enjoy doing)
2. skills (what you're good at doing—due to innate tendencies wired into you at birth or developed through experience and training)
3. finances (what pays the bills)[14]

Our best, most rewarding work will encompass the greatest overlap of these factors.

William Warren has found that overlap in the profession of graphic recording. Before founding The Sketch Effect, he held an enviable job at a company with one of the lowest corporate turnover rates, Chick-fil-A. As Jordan Raynor relates in his book *Called to Create,* Warren loved his job, the people he worked with, and the good compensation. But a factor was missing: Warren wasn't tapping into his lifelong passion for illustration.

Warren explained that ever since he could hold a pencil, he had been drawing comic strips and editorial cartoons:

> When I was in high school, I would sit in class and draw in the margins of my textbooks, creating my own animated flip-books. . . . While I loved my work at Chick-fil-A . . . I have always wanted to start a business where I could combine my passions for illustration and communicating big ideas.[15]

When Warren learned about a relatively new practice called graphic recording—"where an illustrator listens to a speaker at an event and, in real-time, sketches images and text that summarizes the speaker's message"—he taught himself the skill and began using it both on the job (in meetings) and at church during sermons.[16] From there, The Sketch Effect was born, and he was able to leave Chick-fil-A and devote himself full time to something he is both excellent at and loves to do.

Not everyone will start a company. Many simply can't afford to be as flexible or risky in their job pursuits as Warren and Harrison were. We *can* become too idealistic about work, forgetting that even if we land our dream job, we will still face frustrations and difficulties. I (Jenny) love to work from home writing and editing, but I still experience the labor pains that come with birthing a book. While Christ's sacrifice has undone the curse of the fall ultimately, we still experience its effects. But we can still look for work that taps into our God-given uniqueness, even if we end up only pursuing it on the side or in a volunteer or leisure capacity.

Tool 7 is designed to help you identify an overlap of passion, skills, and finances in *your* life. You may find this tool especially useful if you are currently in a work-related transition (e.g., job hunting as a new graduate, considering changing careers, or determining what to do in retirement).

We recommend combining this tool with tool 8 (the Hartman Value Profile [HVP]). The HVP is a valuable assessment to help you better understand yourself in terms of how you engage your work as well as your readiness for work-related change (such as retiring or changing careers). Ironically, the HVP itself was invented by Robert S. Hartman, who made a significant midlife career transition. After winning Walt Disney's highest reward, he quit Disney because the work wasn't fulfilling for him and went on to become the original theorist of the field of scientific axiology (the science of value), in which the HVP is rooted.

As you complete these two tools, remember they are simply tools. God gives us much freedom (within boundaries), and there is no substitute for the counsel and guidance of the Spirit of God in our lives. God's ultimate goal is to shape our character and to reach others through *whatever* work we do.

TOOL 7: PASSION AND COMPETENCE: FINDING YOUR IDEAL OVERLAP

The work that will bring us the most fulfillment and others the most blessing encompasses the greatest overlap of our skills and passions— while also meeting our material and financial needs. This tool is designed to help you find this ideal overlap.[17] Return to this tool periodically (annually or when you grow discontent with your work) to see if there are adjustments you should make.

Note that step 1 is included as a component of tool 2. This entire tool (all steps) may take several hours to complete.

Four Steps

Step 1: Look back. Review your life in five- or ten-year increments. List accomplishments or activities from each period. You can also list other achievements or activities (that span longer periods) in a separate list.

Step 2: Select. Taking your lists from step 1, mark the items that represent those that were or are most important to you (i.e., ones that you're proud of or that represent things you most enjoyed). After doing so, narrow the marked ones down to the four to ten that mean the most to you (preferably sampling from various periods of your life, not only recent years).

Step 3: Describe. Write your top accomplishments or activities along with a short description of each as well as the reason it is important to you.

Step 4: Map it out. Use the blank diagram that follows (fig. 5.1) and transfer the items from step 3 to the boxes associated with the top two circles (passion, competency). Then complete the other box related to the third circle (pays the bills). Finally, jot down your thoughts on the personal reflection questions.

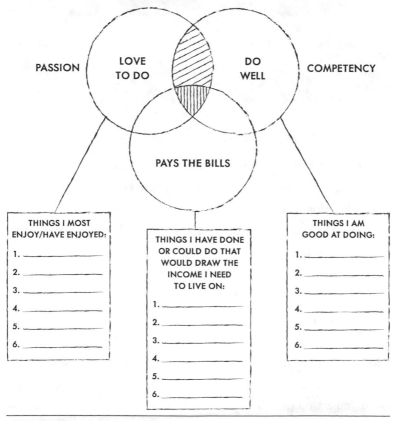

Figure 5.1. Mapping passion and competence

Personal Reflection

✦ What items overlap from the top two circles (passion and competency)?

✦ Of the items you just listed, which ones also show up in your list under the third circle (income—what pays the bills)?

✦ How might you merge the overlapping items in your life

• in your job (if you're still working)?

• in unpaid/volunteer work, such as at church, for a ministry, or in the community?

TOOL 8: ASSESSING YOUR VALUES, DECISION STYLE, AND READINESS FOR CHANGE USING THE HARTMAN VALUE PROFILE

The Hartman Value Profile is not a personality test like Myers-Briggs or the DISC Profile (though if you like those kinds of tests, you will probably enjoy this one too). This tool is an assessment instrument developed by Christian philosopher Robert S. Hartman in the mid-twentieth century.

A test that you can take for free in fifteen minutes or less, the Hartman Value Profile (HVP) is designed primarily to help you understand what you value and in turn to illuminate how you make decisions, choices, and judgments. Results are broken down into two parts—one related more to *doing* in the external world (how your values and judgments affect how you work) and the second to *being* (who you are on the inside). The test even has spiritual implications, with its concepts of values and judgment being rooted in the Old

Testament idea of wisdom (*hokma*) and the New Testament idea of discernment (*sophia*), which Paul saw as a spiritual gift.

The HVP will help you understand your life and yourself in the present; results can vary over your lifetime (since values and decision-making styles change), and they can even differ from one year to the next. The HVP can specifically help you answer questions related to

✦ your ability to handle life changes or transitions

✦ your readiness to retire or to move to a new phase in your career/work

✦ whether you are headed for a personal crisis (midlife or anytime) or if you're already in a crisis (or recovering from one) aspects of your decision-making style that may be helping or hurting you

✦ frustrations, recurrent troubles, or nagging dissatisfaction in your personal or work life

✦ personal tendencies that may be causing you to shoot yourself in the foot

The Hartman Value Profile is unlike personality tests in several ways, starting with the spiritual commitment of its founder. The HVP is based on a branch of philosophy called axiology rather than on Freudian-based psychology. In addition the HVP will result in a mathematically valid score that is objective, unlike subjective personality tests. And results don't tend to stay static—therefore, it's good to complete the test more than once.

You can take the HVP at gladwoodllc.com/recalibrate. In addition to a free standard report of your results using the "Byrum Method" (Steve Byrum was a first-generation student of Hartman himself—it's truest to the original intent of the HVP), as a reader of *Recalibrate Your Life*, you will also receive an exclusive "Readiness for Change" report. This special report pulls out certain aspects of the HVP results that speak directly to life change. If you're in the middle of a life transition right now, we recommend you take the test now and again six months to a year from now.

Although it's optional, for a fee you can add a half-hour consultation session with an expert who will help you interpret your results after you receive them. (We highly recommend doing this because it tends to be illuminating and helps you know what to do with your results.)

Note: An expanded version of this tool, including stories of how the HVP has helped others, is available online at recalibrateyourlife.org.

DOES OUR WORK ENDURE?

We work for God and his glory, and part of the way we glorify him is by pursuing work that blends our unique, God-given background, skills, and passions. But a question still lingers: Does the content or fruit of our labor endure? And if not, how do we stay motivated to work well?

Consider creation itself—the work of God's hands. The Bible tells us this world is passing away and will one day be superseded by a new heaven and a new earth. Yet, even though the flowers and grass of this earth fade within days, he still makes them grow beautifully. We don't see shoddy work anywhere in the universe. Instead, every single aspect of this passing world is fine-tuned to perfection. A gorgeous sunset lasts but minutes, but God still bothers to paint the sky with elaborate strokes of color. An exquisitely designed flower blooms only a few days before its petals wilt and fall off. Why? To reflect his beauty and perfection, and to spur us to marvel at his work (Mark 7:37).

Likewise, the work his image-bearers do may pass away in terms of the tangible, temporal product or results, but if that work is done in a Christian spirit, it has a spiritual, eternal effect that lasts forever: "In the Lord, your labor is not in vain," Paul promises (1 Corinthians 15:58). The chicken sandwich a cashier served us at lunch may be digested within hours, but how that cashier served us and the excellence with which that sandwich was made has the potential to deliver a lasting impression. The legal contracts or court cases settled by a lawyer will ultimately expire, but the souls of those involved in those contracts or cases *are* eternal, and how we conduct our work with them has a long-lasting bearing on them and on how they see our Creator. Trash truck drivers collect trash every week only to have to return to empty the very same trash cans the next week, but the excellence with which they do their job points to the excellence of the One who created a world of order and beauty.

What about ministry work? you may wonder. *Won't that work endure beyond this life?* The answer is *yes* if that work is done "in the Lord." But even ministry work can become wrongly focused or be done with the wrong attitude (1 Corinthians 3:12-15). Whether we're selling widgets, at home raising children, or preaching from a pulpit, all work must be done with an attitude of submission to God—for his praise and approval alone, not for the visible results. Moreover, we cannot force the growth of enduring fruit from our labors. Only God can. We do our part of sowing and watering, but in the end God owns the results.

RECALIBRATING

Let's be honest: work in the twenty-first century looks much different than it did in biblical times and even two hundred years ago. Workers today hold an average of twelve or more jobs during their lifetime. Most don't think twice about changing jobs if it will gain them a higher income or greater flexibility and personal benefits.

Others have chronicled the history and changing nature of work at length (especially the effects of the Industrial Revolution and later the digital revolution); we will not seek to repeat those efforts here. The bottom line is that there are wonderful aspects of working in the twenty-first century, and there are difficult, depressing, dehumanizing, even soul-killing aspects. Some people do find their work deeply satisfying. Others simply muddle through until weekends and holidays (when "real life" happens). Most of us fall somewhere between those two extremes. For all of us, even the most fulfilling work on earth will eventually leave us a little empty if we do not regularly recalibrate our perspective and return to a mindset of stewardship and worship.

The Covid-19-related lockdowns in 2020 and 2021 led many people to reevaluate their work situations and overall priorities in life. (The same thing occurred, to a lesser degree, in the wake of the global financial crisis of 2007–2008.) Recalibrating in the area of work, like in other areas, may be forced on us by external factors, or it may be voluntary. Regardless, the question of work centers on how we use one precious resource: time. *We can never get time back, and none of us knows how much of it we have left.* Numbering our days includes numbering our workdays—and our work hours.

There are only three options when recalibrating:

1. Stay in your current work situation and change nothing.

2. Stay in your current work situation but approach it differently.

3. Change (get out of) your current work situation (i.e., by getting a new job, quitting, or retiring).

Everyone's situation is unique, but we hope the following tips and assessment (in tool 9) will help shape your perspective and inform your next steps.

THREE TIPS FOR EVALUATING YOUR WORK

1. Don't be overeager to quit or retire. Work is good—created by God. Study after study shows that those who retire, especially those who retire early, regardless of preexisting health issues, have increased mortality rates over those who keep working. This statistic underscores the fact that human beings were *made* to work. We were not made to remain idle. Adam was immediately put to work tending the Garden of Eden. Since then, though work is now under the curse, it remains the pattern God established for us—not because we are under a certain, artificially determined age threshold set by our society but because *working is part of what it means to be human.*

Work is often hard because of the sinful world we live in. But you will encounter hard things whether you're working or not. And God has the power to redeem our work, even to bring us (and others) joy and blessing, through our work. At the same time work isn't everything, and there is an appropriate time to scale back our work activities—both to make room for others to step into our roles and to tend to the health of ourselves and our loved ones.

To recalibrate, check your attitude about your current work by reminding yourself *why and for whom* you work.

2. Don't neglect people. The souls of our family and friends are eternal, and relationships are the currency of heaven. Our friend Russ Crosson writes in his excellent book *Your Life . . . Well Spent,* "I'm convinced that in modern society the most common and greatest threat to a balanced life occurs because of the tension between family and work."[18] His keen observation stems from years of experience working with families and from reading the regrets of both them and well-known historical figures ranging from Billy Graham to Garth Brooks. Crosson advises parents of young children, "The children's first ten years are the most critical. If you're making enough [income] now, the extra time may be more valuable than the extra money."[19] Of course, even those who aren't parents can take such advice to heart: Working hard is good, but spending too much time (which we can never get back) solely for income can be a presumptuous move—the exact opportunities and encounters we have today will never return to us again. Money is *for* something, a means to an end. And as believers, if the pursuit of wealth is consistently diminishing our ability to tend to our vertical relationship with God and our horizontal relationships with others, then we need to recalibrate.

To recalibrate we need to remind ourselves of the priority of relationships and God's Word (the two things in this life that carry over into the next).

3. Don't neglect rest and leisure. Besides relationships, rest and leisure can also fall by the wayside when we are due for a recalibration in the area of work. By leisure, we're referring to activities that bring some pleasure (without overindulgence) and that are done freely (not because of any obligation to carry them out); they may even be an amalgam of work and play. Given that God's presence is surrounded by "eternal pleasures" (Psalm 16:11 NIV), pleasure and fun are not outlawed for the Christian. Indeed, our heavenly Father is not a miserly old Scrooge (contrary to his reputation among some) but is pleased to give us gifts that will bring us joy.

Rest, likewise, has an important place in the Christian life. When we rest from our work, we follow the pattern of our Creator himself, who rested from his work on the seventh day of creation. Rest is also the secret to productivity the rest of the week, enabling us to manage stress, work more efficiently and creatively, and maintain a proper perspective of who is really in control. Psalm 127:2 says,

> It is in vain that you rise up early
>   and go late to rest,
> eating the bread of anxious toil;
>   for he gives to his beloved sleep.

We are to "work heartily, as for the Lord" (Colossians 3:23), but we are also to trust him to provide for us. It is an act of worship to lay down our work at night—even if it's incomplete—and get the sleep he made our bodies to need.

To recalibrate, we need to recognize when we are neglecting rest and leisure, confess our sin, and ask God to help us properly prioritize work in relation to other aspects of life. We may need to *schedule* times of rest and leisure into our calendar to ensure it happens. We will often benefit from strategizing with a spouse or roommate. For example, I (Ken) give my wife veto power before I make new commitments, to help me avoid the temptation to overcommit.

Work, leisure, and rest. All three are necessary. And in all three, the orientation of our hearts is what matters most to God. During and after times of transition it's easy for one of these to get thrown out of whack. May we always be willing to confess our sinful tendencies—whether it's toward idolatry and overwork or laziness and apathy—and to return to the perspective and priorities of our heavenly Master.

. . . .
READ AND REFLECT ON
Colossians 3:17-24
. . . .

Consider memorizing verse 23

Prayer: Lord, may I have eyes to see how you view work and how you desire to glorify yourself through the work I do, whether I get financially compensated for it or not. May I submit my activities to you. Help me to shine your light in whatever work I do. And may I follow your model of resting periodically, in an attitude of trust in you as my provider. Amen.

TOOL 9: WORK-LIFE BALANCE ASSESSMENT

This assessment is for anyone but will be especially helpful to those who are currently working.[20] After you take it, spend some time recalibrating in the areas you need to. Remind yourself of the points in this chapter and strategize some concrete steps forward.

✦ Do you have (time) margin in your schedule, or is it usually crammed full?

Possible remedy: Schedule time in your calendar for leisure and rest, just as you would any other appointment. Have someone else keep you accountable for sticking to that schedule if necessary. Start with ten minutes a day or one hour per week for each.

Note: *Leisure* is time spent doing something like a hobby that you enjoy for its own sake (not because it produces something); *rest* involves no set activities or plans (e.g., taking a nap, watching the birds in your backyard, or lying in a hammock at a park).

✦ Do you regularly overcommit or take on work or tasks that you later regret or begrudge doing?

Possible remedy: Write set criteria for accepting new assignments or invitations. If you're married, one criterion might be to give your spouse veto power before you accept a new commitment.

✦ Does work (either by your own choice or because of your employer's demands on you) often take up time you would normally spend with God or in Christian fellowship (e.g., church)?

Possible remedy: Determine a consistent time and place you meet with God each day. Start with ten minutes and increase the time gradually. Avoid committing to any optional (leisure) activity that will encroach on your church's weekly worship gathering time.

✦ If you're married or live with children or other relatives, does work (either by your own choice or because of your employer's demands on you) often take up time you would normally spend with family?

Possible remedy: Determine family time each week that is nonnegotiable (for example, sharing dinner and a daily walk, reading aloud as a family before bed either nightly or for a more extended time one evening a week, attending kids' or grandkids' ball games or other activities). Tell your family about your plan to help you stick to it. You might be surprised at the effect your efforts have on the peace and unity of your household.

✦ Does your work often cause you to get less sleep than you need?

Possible remedy: Have a hard stop to the end of your workday and make any exceptions rare.

✦ Are you working more, often to the neglect of other areas of life (spirituality, relationships, rest), with the mindset that you will earn enough now to relax more later or even retire early?

Possible remedy: Choose a slower career path; plan to work until you're older rather than being in a big hurry to retire. If you have the option, choose extra vacation time over salary increases.

✦ Are you often overwhelmed by your work?

Possible remedy: Ask or hire others to help you and free up some of your time (even if it means a reduction in your income and the work not getting done in the same way you would like it done).

✦ Do you work from home and feel like work has taken over your personal/home life?

Possible remedy: Designate a workspace in a protected area of your home. Ensure everyone in the household is aware of the rules of this place (e.g., when it's okay to enter and when it's not). These boundaries are especially important if you have young kids at home. If you have a variable-time job, where you don't have to work a certain number of hours but simply have to get the job done, develop set work hours, and stick to them (with exceptions being rare). On the flip side, if you have a fixed-income job (with fixed hours), don't jump ship *too* eagerly; a variable-time job (even if it makes more money) may not be a better fit for you *yet*, as it may too easily encroach on family time.

✦ Do you find yourself considering changing jobs/careers often?

Possible remedy: Change careers only to better fulfill your purpose or maximize your time flexibility, not solely to make more money. Review ways to recalibrate and improve your approach to your current job.

✦ Do you feel persistently dissatisfied or unfulfilled in your work?

Possible remedy: Find a different job that aligns with your lifelong calling from God (see part two for more on this), and live within the income it provides. If that is not an option, then examine your attitudes toward your current job and seek change in whatever ways you can.

✦ Do you feel pressured at work to conform to views (or engage in activities) that run counter to biblical truth?

Possible remedy: Marginalization and other soft forms of persecution have occurred for decades, but we are now seeing an intensifying demand in workplaces to conform to prevailing cultural perspectives on issues such as gender and race. Some job environments have become so toxic that followers of Christ have had little choice but to count the cost, quit their jobs (or open themselves to being fired), and find work elsewhere.[21] If quitting isn't an option, pray for boldness rather than timidity, and for the courage to stay strong in your convictions in the face of hostility. Pray that you will be wise as a serpent and innocent as a dove (Matthew 10:16), knowing when to speak up and when to stay quiet. Seek to please God over people every single day (Galatians 1:10). And seek out other believers in your workplace with whom you can band together.

Next Steps

Make a list of areas in which you need to recalibrate and concrete steps for how you will do so.

CHAPTER FIVE

DEVELOPING A BETTER VISION OF RETIREMENT

[The righteous] still bear fruit in old age;
they are ever full of sap and green.

PSALM 92:14

I magine a marathon runner training for months and persevering through most of the race only to drop out at mile twenty-five. Sure, any runner is exhausted by that point—his or her body feeling like it will suddenly fail and collapse (some do). But with 95 percent of the race complete and just over a mile left to the finish line, why would that runner bow out then with so much already invested and the end in sight?

After years of mentoring, teaching, and discipling many talented and successful adults, I (Ken) see this same situation in the race of life. After achieving the greatest capacity in terms of time, financial resources, skills, and knowledge, too many people go off into retirement land with no more definite plans than leisurely pursuits and perhaps a little extra time with family. Followers of Jesus who have been active in the church for years suddenly bench themselves, ceding ministry roles to those with more energy and depriving the next generation of wisdom accumulated over a lifetime.

To be sure, the effects of aging are real and can hinder us in either small or drastic ways. At some point, unless we graduate to the next life first, we *will* face the difficult transition to that stage that is known as old age. This transition happens gradually but can be accelerated by a sudden event or crisis. Regardless, it becomes easy to assume— often unconsciously—that, once we reach a certain age, our best, most fruitful days are behind us. That we are, somehow, *less useful* to God.

But what if that's not the way our Creator sees our mature years? What if he wants to use us in our latter days as much as, or even more than, he used us in our youthful vitality? *What if what we lack in vigor and youthfulness, we make up for in experience and wisdom?*

We believe there is indeed a better way, a better vision, that is hope-filled while not discounting the realities of diminished capacities and energy.

A Tale of Caution

Phil Burgess (friend of Ken's and author of *Reboot!*) retired at age sixty with a somewhat stereotypical ideal of retirement:

> Now I could do all the things I wanted to do. I could read more books . . . reflect on and rekindle old relationships, and revisit old dreams. My wife and I could go sailing on the Chesapeake Bay or down the Intracoastal Waterway to Florida. . . . I could more regularly attend my local Rotary Club . . . and get more involved in community service.[1]

Burgess's vision evaporated quickly, and (he concedes) it was his fault.

Entering his postcareer life on autopilot, he began to find "things to do . . . to resurrect a sense of purpose" to his days. Whether it was volunteering for a local school or speaking abroad or helping a friend start a new nonprofit, he received and accepted one opportunity after another, sometimes offering his time for free. While many of these activities harnessed a lifetime of expertise and made him feel good, he says, "The commitments piled up. All of a sudden, in the space of a few months, I didn't have time to go sailing, read books, or drive over to the university to have dinner with my kids and catch up with their lives. After just a few months of retirement . . . I was . . . busier than ever, and it wasn't all good."[2]

A few more months passed, and Burgess attended a workshop on transitions. The teaching impressed on him the importance of recalibration (though he doesn't use that term): "I learned of the need for individuals . . . to make sure the transition process includes a *time-out* to step back, reassess, redefine, and rethink where they've been and where they are going."[3]

As part of his recalibration process, Burgess revisited his unique gifts and calling, assessing them in light of his new stage.[4] Not only did he regain his balance and begin to enjoy life more again, but he wrote a book to help others prepare to reboot (e.g., start a second career) in retirement.

Without such a reevaluation we will not have a well-defined vision or script (as Burgess calls it) to guide our later years. As a result we will not only be prone to some of the same pitfalls discussed in chapter five, but we will wear out fast (probably faster than in our younger days), and we may miss the chance to make a singular impact in a particular area God wants us to focus on.

At this point let us emphasize that younger readers shouldn't tune out. *Even if retirement is still on the distant horizon*, the way you view the latter part of your life affects how you live, work, plan for the future, and manage your resources today. So please stick with us!

MODERN RETIREMENT

The concept most of us have of retirement is quite new—dating back less than a century. It was spawned largely by the changing nature of work due to industrialization along with increasing life expectancies and a few other factors. Another important factor was the introduction of the pension in 1875 (by American Express).

Although the practice of offering pensions began gaining momentum in the early 1900s, as of 1932 most Americans (more than 85 percent) still didn't enjoy the luxury of a paid retirement. The assumption was that you would keep working as long as necessary and as long as you were able. Then came the Great Depression, triggering a series of policy acts designed to alleviate growing unemployment. Public pensions came to be seen as "a major tool to get young men working again." How? By getting "more older men [to] retire" (this was, of course, before women constituted a large portion of the workforce).[5] Enter the Social Security Act.

At first, Social Security hardly kept retirees out of poverty, but over time the country emerged out of the Depression and more companies could offer workers supplementary pensions in exchange for loyal service. The public perception of retirement changed as well, buoyed by public relations and advertising efforts. Before long, the image of a retiree had transformed "from a cat-food-eating granny to a tanned and healthy couple, living in an idyllic villa and playing lots of golf—or climbing an ice-covered mountain. Retirement became that most desirable of things, a *lifestyle*."[6]

Fast forward to the early 2000s and this picturesque ideal of retirement has most likely seen its heyday. As early as 1995 one article was predicting, "The end of retirement as we know it is nigh, even for people who don't think retiring is a lousy idea."[7] Social Security is now in full-blown crisis (and has been for years), thanks to increasing life expectancies (along with a failure to adjust the age people begin collecting it), dramatically expanded coverages, and an exploding population of retirees in comparison to the number of workers paying into the program. On top of this, private companies' handling of retirement benefits has changed. The days of employees being paid a certain percentage (often as much as half or even more) of their salary at retirement—known as a defined-benefits plan (or private pension)—are largely over, replaced by defined-contribution plans (to which the employee designates a portion of his or her salary each month, *sometimes* but not always accompanied by an employer match).[8] Add population dynamics and a host of financial and other economic woes to the mix, and the picture of retirement today has become much less rosy, especially for the up-and-coming generations.

While a small percentage of individuals are still wealthy enough to retire and enjoy a period of leisurely retirement, this situation is becoming less common—and less certain even for those who have diligently saved. Those who have built handsome retirement accounts face the prospect of savings being wiped out overnight (as happened to some in 2020), often forcing the postponement of retirement until markets recover. According to one index, half of American retirees in 2021 were at risk of not having enough money to sustain their preretirement standard of living.[9] Pensions are enjoyed by only one-third of retirees, and that percentage continues to decline. Personal retirement savings are widely reported as insufficient—with a quarter of all Americans reporting *zero* retirement savings in 2020.[10] The result? More retirees find themselves returning to work to supplement retirement income. According to retirement statistics, most (89 percent) US adults work until age seventy-five. In addition, half of Americans sixty-five and older have an annual income lower than $24,224—far less than most people need to cover their daily living expenses (making supplemental income a necessity for many in this age group).[11]

We could throw out many more statistics and trends, but you get the picture. Even if you think the modern idea of retirement is a good one, it may not be feasible for you—or your children or grandchildren. Prior generations enjoyed a windfall "likely never to be seen again."[12] The reality is this:

> *The retirement ideal that has been sold to many people for the past sixty-plus years is not attainable by the vast majority of Americans, and it is even less attainable in the future.*

Moreover, researchers have demonstrated health benefits to continuing to work, further confirming that even those who can afford to retire should consider their retirement years not as a period of idle leisure and free time for them to spend as they wish but as a time to continue to be fruitful contributors to society, albeit often in new and different ways than when they were younger.

Of course, there are much better reasons to recalibrate your approach to retirement beyond practical and logistical ones. But, perhaps not coincidentally, all of what we have just described points back to the wisdom of God's Word as a blueprint for the later years of our lives.

RETIREMENT IN THE BIBLE

One of the Israelites chosen to spy out the Promised Land, Caleb was one of the only two spies who believed God's promise that the Israelites would take possession of the land (despite how intimidating its inhabitants appeared). Three times Scripture tells us Caleb followed God fully (or wholeheartedly). In Joshua 14 we find him in what we assume were his twilight years:

> Now, behold, I am this day eighty-five years old. I am still as strong today as I was in the day that Moses sent me; my strength now is as my strength was then, for war and for going and coming. So now give me this hill country [Hebron] of which the LORD spoke on that day, for you heard on that day how the Anakim were there,

with great fortified cities. It may be that the LORD will be with me, and I shall drive them out just as the Lord said. (Joshua 14:10-12)

Caleb does indeed take Hebron. We don't know how much longer he lived after that. But we do know that at a time when most people think it's too late to do anything big and productive, Caleb still had a ministry mindset. He was enthusiastic, gutsy, and passionate about proving what the Lord could do through one who trusted him completely. Granted, not all of us have his physical vitality in old age, but this aspect does not seem to play the central role in Caleb's spiritually gung-ho attitude; rather it was his faith in God's ability to use him and to fulfill his promises that stands out.

A survey of the rest of Scripture reveals similar accounts of God's people—Adam, Abraham, Moses, Joshua, the apostle John—remaining active in ministry in old age, to the very end of their lives. The only place in the Bible that gives any grounds for the concept of retirement is found in the book of Numbers. There, we see the following description given about the Levites—the priests given special duties related to the care of and worship in the tabernacle and temple:

> This applies to the Levites: from twenty-five years old and upward they shall come to do duty in the service of the tent of meeting. And from the age of fifty years they shall withdraw from the duty of the service and serve no more. They minister to their brothers in the tent of meeting by keeping guard, but they shall do no service. (Numbers 8:24-26)

These priests were to serve in their unique roles for twenty-five years and then retire. But notice the definition of retirement: they were no longer to carry out their same service, but they were still to "keep guard" and "minister to their brothers." Their responsibilities changed; they were no longer doing the same duties. But the Levites were still involved in God's work, serving side by side with—providing support to—those who held official roles.

The example of the Levites is certainly not prescriptive, but taken with the rest of Scripture we can confidently say this:

> *Although we may retire from a job or profession, God's call for us to work for his kingdom and bear spiritual fruit does not come with an expiration date.*

As an outworking of growing intimacy with God, we are always to pursue activities that enrich not only ourselves but also others around us. Earlier, we referenced Psalm 92, which paints a picture of the righteous still bearing fruit in old age (v. 14). Here are a few more verses advocating for a strong finish to our lives:

✦ "We have come to share in Christ, if indeed we hold our original confidence firm to the end" (Hebrews 3:14).

✦ "We desire each one of you to show the same earnestness to have the full assurance of hope until the end" (Hebrews 6:11).

✦ "Hold fast to what you have until I come. The one who conquers and who keeps my works until the end, to him I will give authority over the nations" (Revelation 2:25-26).

Although these verses don't advocate a dizzying pace of activity in retirement (as Phil Burgess found himself in), neither do they suggest we should do nothing but kick back on a beach in Florida or play golf each week for *years on end*. This isn't a knock on leisure in general (or on beach bumming or golfing in particular); Scripture certainly does not bar Christians from pleasurable activities or seasons of greater rest and leisure. Yet God's Word is clear that there is always work to be done for God's kingdom—always more souls to reach with the gospel. A gradual fade-out, fizzle, or time of wilting is simply not presented as an option for a follower of Jesus. Instead, we are to die to ourselves and live for Christ, remaining engaged in ministry to the very end of our earthly pilgrimages. *This* is what we mean by rejecting the world's idea of retirement—not that people should never retire from their jobs or careers.

Our God-given purpose will have a multiplicity of manifestations throughout life. Because of the deepening nature of faith, wisdom, and discipline in the Christian life, the trajectory of our lives can be seen as a continual *winding up* (culminating in our graduation to the next life) instead of a *winding down*.

Horst Schulze spent over sixty years building a hotel empire that made him a legend in the hospitality industry. The chair emeritus of Capella Hotel Group easily could have coasted into retirement and never worked a day in his life again. Instead, he has continued to use his unique experience and talents by developing a template that can be applied in a variety of industries (not just hotel chains) and provides consulting services around the world. Horst's ongoing engagement isn't just a hunger for continued influence, however; it reflects his lifelong calling to create a culture of excellence. This culture—marked by genuine care and service, treating people like they truly matter (because they do)—has a functional expression, but it is ultimately rooted in this one man's commitment to spiritual (Christian), moral, relational, theoretical, and functional excellence (see fig. 6.1).[13]

Russ Crosson and his colleagues at Ronald Blue Trust have a term for people like Schulze: a sage. A sage is "a mature or a venerable man/woman sound in prudence and good judgment; respected through age, character, attainment—someone to

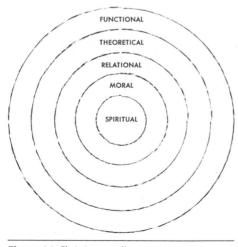

Figure 6.1. Christian excellence

emulate and learn from."[14] A sage may *also* be an expert, but the two are not the same. While an expert merely impresses others, a sage draws people closer to God through their accumulated wisdom.

OLDER ISN'T BAD

There's a saying that "good decisions come from experience, and most of that comes from bad decisions." In short, we learn a lot from our setbacks, and if we develop good judgment, it usually happens after a lifetime of learning—often the *hard way* type of learning. No wonder wisdom is associated with the aged (even though it's not strictly reserved for those advanced in years). And no wonder many cultures (especially those in the East) have traditionally held the elderly of their society in the *highest* regard.

In *Successful Aging* Daniel Levitin joins a chorus of voices advocating for a shift in mindset about the elderly and getting older. While acknowledging the limitations of aging, he also highlights various benefits of getting older, one of which is improved "crystallized intelligence." Psychologist Raymond Cattell first defined this type of intelligence, which he distinguished from "fluid intelligence."

> Cattell defined fluid intelligence as the ability to reason, analyze, and solve novel problems—what we commonly think of as raw intellectual horsepower. Innovators typically have an abundance of fluid intelligence. It is highest relatively early in adulthood and diminishes starting in one's 30s and 40s. This is why tech entrepreneurs, for instance, do so well so early. . . . Crystallized intelligence, in contrast, is the ability to use knowledge gained in the past. Think of it as possessing a vast library and understanding how to use it. It is the essence of wisdom. Because crystallized intelligence relies on an accumulating stock of knowledge, it tends to increase through one's 40s, and does not diminish until very late in life.[15]

Increased crystallized intelligence is just one reason later life can be, as Levitin puts it, a time of "culmination instead of denouement . . . a period of blossoming, a resurgence of life that does not chase after our younger years, but instead embraces the gifts that time can bring."[16] As a neuroscientist Levitin concedes that people "vary considerably" in the ways and rates they age, especially in terms of cognitive abilities.[17] However, his field of research shows that although our brains' neuroplasticity (its ability to rewire and adapt) lessens as we age, it can still occur and be nurtured through our lifestyle. There's a physiological explanation behind this advice:

> When we feel rejected or underappreciated . . . our bodies react . . . by releasing cortisol, the stress hormone. Cortisol is very useful if you need to invoke the fight-or-flight response, . . . but it is not so useful when you're dealing with longer-term psychological challenges such as loss of respect. . . . In contrast, when we're actively engaged and excited about life, our levels of mood-enhancing hormones such as serotonin and dopamine increase.[18]

Levitin adds, "No matter what age we are, our brains are always changing in response to pressures from genes, culture, and opportunity."[19] Consequently, we can pursue certain practices to minimize the negative effects of age, maximize its positives, and ease the transitions that come with older age. These practices range from learning (or maintaining) a manual skill to purposely engaging with new people to traveling to a new place.

Levitin's concern seems to be focused largely on *this* world, but his observations are nonetheless poignant in the context of the spiritual reality that encompasses our earthly experiences. *It's not all downhill from here,* he is essentially saying. *We can recalibrate at any age or stage.* We can see the latter part of life positively, as a season of new opportunity, albeit fraught with challenges and blessings just like other stages (a direct contrast from Mitch's view of life in that scene in *City Slickers*). Furthermore, when the young and old commingle more, each sharing the blessings of their life stage, everyone benefits—individuals and society as a whole.

"What would it mean for all of us to think of the elderly as a resource rather than a burden?" Levitin asks. "It would mean harnessing a human resource that is being wasted, or, at best, underutilized," he continues. "It would promote stronger family bonds and stronger bonds of friendship among us all. It would mean that important decisions at all scales, from personal matters to intergenerational agreements, would be informed by experience and reason, along with the perspective that old age brings."[20]

It would also, we might add, result in faith and godly wisdom being shared more between generations.

SAGES OF SCRIPTURE: A LESSON FROM ISRAEL'S HISTORY

We see this very lesson when we contrast two leaders in the Old Testament. In 1 Kings we read about the "folly" of King Rehoboam. He has just become king, and the people are asking him to "lighten the hard service" and "heavy yoke" his father, King Solomon, had placed on them. In his decision making King Rehoboam consults two sets of advisers about how he should respond to the people's request.

> King Rehoboam took counsel with the old men, who had stood before Solomon his father while he was yet alive, saying, "How do you advise me to answer this people?" And they said to him, "If you will be a servant to this people today and serve them, and speak good words to them when you answer them, then they will be your servants forever." But he abandoned the counsel that the old men gave him and took counsel with the young men who had grown up with him and stood before him. (1 Kings 12:6-8)

In short, the young men advised Rehoboam to be an even harsher ruler than his father—thus turning down the people's request. Needless to say, forsaking the counsel of the sages did not go well for Rehoboam. Besides being forced to flee Jerusalem, there was turmoil and rebellion during his reign, and the kingdom of Israel was ultimately divided on his watch.

By contrast, if we turn back to Exodus 18, we find Moses, post exodus from Egypt, trying his best to lead the Israelites. His father-in-law, Jethro, notices the people coming to Moses to help them resolve their disputes. Jethro has the insight to see that Moses is going to suffer burnout if he keeps his current pace. To his son-in-law, Jethro says,

> You and the people with you will certainly wear yourselves out, for the thing is too heavy for you. You are not able to do it alone. . . . Look for able men from all the people, men who fear God, who are trustworthy and hate a bribe, and place such men over the people as chiefs of thousands, of hundreds, of fifties, and of tens. And let them judge the people at all times. Every great matter they shall bring to you, but any small matter they shall decide themselves. So it will be easier for you, and they will bear the burden with you. If you do this, God will direct you, you will be able to endure, and all this people also will go to their place in peace. (Exodus 18:18, 21-23)

What comes next is key. Moses could've been stubborn like Rehoboam would be later (and as many new leaders are). He could've resisted the advice of this (presumably) older man, insistent that he could manage things just fine, thank you.[21] Instead, the Scripture tells us, "Moses listened to the voice of his father-in-law and did all that he had said" (Exodus 18:24). From there, although Moses' life was imperfect and undoubtedly filled with challenges, we know this humble, teachable man enjoyed a long life of 120 years and died with the respect of the people—a sage just like his father-in-law.

PRACTICAL CONSIDERATIONS

The first year after retiring was the hardest for Anne. "I felt as though I had lost my identity," she says. "Saying 'retired' was hard—seemed to imply old, out-of-touch, on the shelf . . . no longer an active player."

Though she had been self-employed and most of her meetings had gone virtual, Anne missed being part of a team—having places to go, people to see. The sense of loss was palpable and still is. At the same time God opened new opportunities for her and her husband, Jim (also retired). Anne and Jim began increasing their involvement in an area they had always been called to: ministry to international students. Together, the couple became one of the go-to hosts for gatherings of local university students curious to learn more about Jesus.

"God has filled our home in retirement!" Anne says, adding that, despite challenges, retirement has truly become one of the happiest times in their lives. She loves that she now has the "time, resources, and opportunity" to pursue one of her greatest joys more fully.

Yet Anne emphasizes the reality of *loss* in this stage. Besides the loss of a sense of purpose and identity, other losses associated with retirement might include

+ loss of health, energy, and a sense of physical well-being
+ loss of relationships—friends, spouses, other family members, colleagues
+ loss of a structured schedule and a certain level of daily productivity
+ loss of tangible belongings due to downsizing (often attached to intangible memories)
+ loss of income due to no longer working (or to scaling back on work)

Thus far, we've been establishing the basis for developing a new vision for retirement, one that sees this period of life not as one of inevitable decline but of ongoing engagement, even *culmination* (of impact, wisdom, and maturity) as we prepare to enter our permanent, eternal dwelling place. At the same time we know Anne's experience is not unusual. Aging is, in a sense, a mixed bag.

I (Ken) am in my late seventies and have watched close friends, as well as family members, leave this earth at a growing pace. And although I have been blessed with only minor health setbacks personally so far, I have cared for my bride, Karen, as she has endured considerable diminishment in recent years—both of us reluctantly accepting the limitations it places on our travel and other plans.

Although I have been blessed with an unusual amount of energy, all of us need to dial back on our activities and commitments as we age. Physical limitations (such as loss of hearing, eyesight, or mobility), loss of energy, and shrinking social circles are real and can prevent us from doing the things we most enjoy and from connecting well with others. So, even if *older* isn't bad, it's certainly harder in many ways.

In the face of aging-related challenges it can be helpful to remember that God is interested in quality, not quantity. While we may have some diminished capabilities as we get older, we also bring to the table a wealth of experience and knowledge that we didn't have in our earlier years. In addition, God specializes in multiplying the effects of our actions. Even if we encounter and share his love with just one person each day—like an in-home nurse or a postal worker or a delivery person bringing a package to the door—a seemingly small act can have a large impact. This was Corrie ten Boom's approach. When homebound in old age she didn't think about doing a lot day after day; she thought and prayed about who God wanted her to share him with *today*.

We are shaped by our adversities and weaknesses, and God often works through our weaknesses as much as, if not more than, our strengths (2 Corinthians 12:9-10). From tight finances to physical maladies to relational pains, our sufferings are often the very tools God uses to reach others through us. Our hardships can also create in us a fresh appetite for the eternal and a deeper sense of hope for the joy of our unbounded future (Psalm 119:50, 92).

RECALIBRATING

The experience of old age varies substantially from person to person. For some it's a honeymoon-like stage, full of freedom and flexibility (often buoyed by a comfortable financial cushion). For others, retirement never comes or is only partial. For an increasing number this stage features a reboot—the launch of a second career, either out of necessity or out of a desire to do something one has always wanted to do.[22]

Thankfully, from time immemorial, God has been working in and through people in all stages and conditions. Whether we die young or live to eighty or even longer (cf. Psalm 90:10), so long as we have life and breath, he has—and will fulfill—his purpose for us.

As we go through or approach this unique period of life, asking the following two questions, in combination with tool 10, can help you recalibrate and make necessary adjustments.

1. What opportunities does God want you to see and seize? God calls us to make the most of every opportunity placed before us (Ephesians 5:16). We need not preoccupy ourselves with what we *can't* do in our old age but instead focus on what God is showing us we *can* do. Time is his, not ours (Psalm 31:15). Every minute, every hour, belongs to him.

> *Retirement years aren't* me time *any more*
> *than any other period of our life is.*

This doesn't preclude doing things for pleasure. But even in our leisurely pursuits, we can have an eternal mindset. For example, we can look for a couple to befriend on our river cruise (or other traveling adventure) and be intentional about sharing the gospel with them. Or we can find a younger person to share a hobby with—from tennis or golf to carpentry, gardening, and investing in the stock market—and use the connection to take the relationship to a deeper level, even one of spiritual mentoring. If we're in a more constricted environment, such as an assisted-living community, we can find a meal buddy and develop a friendship and (as the Spirit leads) share Christ with that person.

2. Who does God want you to invest in? The need to treasure people, who are eternal, over things, can come into sharper focus as we advance in years. One temptation as we age (especially as things like hearing loss become a reality) is to withdraw from other people. Although we will likely have to reduce the number of our interactions, doing so too drastically will diminish both our lives and the lives of those in our community. The body of Christ is the context in which we worship and grow, and we need one another to properly recalibrate. Younger people need the wisdom of older generations, and mentoring relationships (whether formal or informal) are one of the key ways to invest in people.

Another important way we can invest in others as we age is to be open and vulnerable (discerningly, of course) about setbacks, pains, and fears. I (Jenny) have been particularly encouraged by my own dad's openness about his struggles as he has dealt with heart disease. Witnessing him wrestle spiritually and physically with an aging body has helped me see that there is a place for sorrow and lament as we grow older, but as our earthly suits wear out, this is also cause for a more radical hope and dependence on God for daily strength and grace. Too often we forget the magnificence of what God is planning for us because we are overly focused on the past or present.

- - - - - - - - - - - - - -
READ AND REFLECT ON
Psalm 92
- - - - - - - - - - - - - -

Consider memorizing verses 12-14

Prayer: Lord, help me approach every day and every year of my life with intentionality—intent on following you and the pattern you have set out in Scripture for your followers rather than the pattern of this world. Enlarge my vision of my retirement years (whether they're here already or many years away); help me see them as a period of abundant opportunity and potential, a time when you can use me in new ways. Amen.

TOOL 10: RETHINKING RETIREMENT: ARE YOU A SAGE OR ON THE ROAD TO BECOMING ONE?

A sage is a mature or venerable man or woman sound in prudence and good judgment, respected through age, character, and attainment.[23] A sage is someone to emulate and learn from, a person who relies on and regularly spends time with God and who, in turn, draws others to God. Though a sage may be an expert (with impressive knowledge and experience in a certain area), an expert is not always a sage. Humility is one of the distinguishing factors between these two roles.

The Ten Characteristics of a Sage

1. *Available* (in the game, ready and willing to be "spent for [people's] souls" [2 Corinthians 12:15])

2. *Humble* (selfless, realizing life and legacy are not about you but about making God known to current and future generations)

3. *Others-focused* (a promoter and encourager of others, supports others and is not jealous, serving as a mentor)

4. *Wisdom* (skill in the art of living, significantly related to knowing and being able to correctly handle God's Word)

5. *Experienced* (possessing good judgment, demonstrating influence and specialized knowledge)

6. *Confident but not competitive* (the focus is on passing down wisdom and providing humble guidance based on experience and unique gifts, not on impressing or showing off; title, income, and position don't matter, nor does always being right)

7. *Holistic thinker* (able to synthesize and see the big picture of life; knows what to sweat and what not to sweat)

8. *Empathetic* (possessing emotional intelligence—soft skills such as gratitude, maturity, and good-naturedness)

9. *Librarian* (a resource to others, having both know-who and know-how)

10. *Good questioner and listener* (care for and attention to others, which leads to their development and learning)

Personal Reflection

✦ Who are some of the sages you have known—people who have influenced you personally and have demonstrated the above characteristics?

✦ Would you consider yourself a sage right now? Why or why not? What characteristics are you strongest in? Weakest?

✦ What steps will you take to become a sage or to grow in your role as a sage? (Specify one or two of the characteristics that you need to focus on.)

✦ Who can you invest in, in a sage role? How? (Note: This may not be a question you can answer yet, depending on your age and life stage.)

PART II

PURPOSE

What Gives
Direction to Life?

CHAPTER SIX

UNDERSTANDING GOD'S PURPOSES

The LORD will fulfill his purpose for me;
your steadfast love, O LORD, endures forever.
Do not forsake the work of your hands.

PSALM 138:8

K eli didn't expect to be returning to school or job hunting in her fifties. Like many transitions, hers was forced on her by adversity. Yet, as with many people, her suffering has drawn her closer to God and has been the very tool he has used to help her uncover and live her unique purpose within his larger purposes.

Before her divorce Keli endured three decades of worsening abuse in her marriage, leading to deep betrayal trauma.

> I learned in the first year of marriage that my husband was addicted to pornography and had an unfaithful heart where he emotionally attached to other women. As the years passed, emotional, sexual, and physical abuse characterized my marriage,

with him disappearing for lengths of time and having affairs, gas-lighting me, and manipulating my relationships with my children. I suffered STDs, anxiety, and clinical depression with two years of fighting suicidal desires. . . . As decades passed, his actions became more abusive with sexual cruelty and coercion, he drained our finances to accounts I didn't have access to, and I was afraid to leave him for fear of custody battles and that he would retaliate.

Keli had homeschooled their three children. When her youngest was in college, she explains, a counselor made it her mission to help Keli become "strong enough to leave" her marriage. Strengthened through a revitalized prayer life (thanks to the counselor), Keli finally stood up to her husband and said enough is enough. She followed God's leading and applied to a nursing program at age fifty. "It took two painful, confusing years to finalize the divorce and two years of nursing school," she says. Upon graduating she was still wrestling with feeling like a failure. But she knew she had to do *something* to support herself. She began attending job workshops and investigating how she might use her nursing degree.

One day she reached out to the ministry Mercy Ships to inquire if they needed any nursing help. They did—immediately. "As soon as I had my vaccinations and visa in hand," she says, "I was on a plane across the ocean to where no one knew my past, my family, or my ex-husband. I could walk in the joys and demands of each day serving."

"Living in lies and deception for decades," Keli says, she was still in shock, but on that ship docked in Togo, "a lot of healing happened"—in her heart and in the physical bodies of those she was serving. She was recalibrating, perhaps without knowing it.

But her journey was far from over. On returning to the United States, Keli moved to be with her aging parents and had difficulty finding a job. The nursing market in her region was flooded, and new graduates were being hired to replace older nurses. She didn't stand a chance, so she fell back on teaching. A labyrinthine career path ensued. At one point she was putting in over sixty hours of work a week for an annual salary of $30,000.

Then Covid-19 hit. At the time Keli was working with senior citizens, but now no senior groups were meeting. So she applied for—and started—a new job all over again. Now working as director of resident care at an assisted-living facility, she was getting closer to finding her niche, but she still wasn't there.

"It took seven years of changes to find 'my place,' all while in my sixth decade of life and watching peers retire," Keli says.

She is now a hospice nurse—a job that beautifully illustrates the merging of a God-given calling and a career.

"I have experienced great pain and confusion," she says, explaining how she knew she'd found her place.

I'm not afraid of pain or death. This world is *not* our home, so joy comes when we come alongside and help each other. I can enter a room where someone is dying and bring some peace [and] comfort. . . . I can live with the eternal perspective and ask the family where they think their loved one is going. . . . I get to combine that with the science of end of life.

Looking back, Keli says she never felt God abandoned her—she had no crisis of faith. But she certainly had doubts about her identity and purpose. Today, while she is still unraveling the confusion of her married life—years of deception aren't easily reconciled—she is in a much better place. God allowed everything she relied on to be stripped away (her husband, her family, her home, and whole social circles), so that only he remained. "God has traveled this life with me and knows me better than any living being on this earth. I feel I'm a participant in the gospel as I bring moments of his hands in my work."

THE PROCESS OF FINDING YOUR PURPOSE

Keli's marriage crisis and divorce inaugurated a transition in her life that she wouldn't wish on anyone. But it also led her to find her unique purpose of bringing hope, comfort, and healing to people at the end of their lives (as well as to their grieving family members). While some transitions are similarly dramatic, many are not. Regardless of whether they're subtle or dramatic, forced on us (like receiving a sudden cancer diagnosis) or anticipated for some time (like having a baby or starting a company), these moments provide the perfect *kairos* opportunities for recalibration.

A major component of recalibration is returning to, or discovering for the first time, a sense of personal purpose in life.

> *Our God-given calling (vocation) can be defined*
> *as our* unchanging reason for being.

It's the essence of who we are, why we're on earth, and what separates us from other humans. Unlike a career, our unique purpose comes with no expiration date; it is lifelong. Although God is always preparing us for our unique purpose (even before we've decided to follow him), that doesn't mean we're aware of it our entire lives. Our understanding and ability to articulate our purpose evolves. Indeed, the way our calling is manifested will be different across our lifetime. Sometimes we even resist it.

Consider the circumstances in which the following biblical characters found their unique purpose in life (ages are approximate):

+ Abraham was called by God around age seventy to realize his purpose of being the progenitor of a people through whom God would bless the world; the promised offspring (Isaac) didn't arrive until Abraham was a hundred years old.

+ Moses was called by God at age eighty to deliver the Hebrew slaves from Egypt, a purpose Moses was reluctant to fulfill.

✦ Paul, as a young (early thirties) rabbinic scholar, learned his purpose—to deliver the gospel to Gentiles and their kings—over the course of a few days, following a dramatic encounter with Jesus on the road to Damascus.

✦ Elisha, when perhaps in his twenties, dropped his farmer's role and agreed to be Elijah's assistant, which led to his role as a prophet.

✦ David was anointed as a teenager to be the next king of Israel.

✦ Jeremiah learned (likely as a teenager) that God had purposed for him to be a prophet while still in his mother's womb.

✦ Elizabeth and Zechariah were "advanced in years" and past child-bearing age when an angel announced they would give birth to the man (John the Baptist) who would prepare the people for the Messiah's arrival.

✦ Mary was only a teenager and her fiancé, Joseph, was perhaps in his early twenties when they were handed the life-changing purpose to be the earthly parents of Jesus Christ.

✦ Anna of Jerusalem, a widow, saw her purpose as praying and worshiping in the temple, which she did into her eighties.

✦ Jesus himself sensed his unique purpose early on (from at least age twelve), and in his early thirties he embarked on fulfilling that purpose publicly.

To this list we could add many more names, from inside and outside of the Bible. The point is that people can and do discover their distinct purpose in life; however, there is no fixed pattern as to when and how that discovery occurs. It may happen when we are younger or (as for Keli) older; it may happen suddenly or gradually; it may happen convincingly or doubtfully; it may be revealed as in a vision or deduced from a long discovery process.

PART OF A LARGER PURPOSE

We cannot discover, understand, and live out our unique purpose apart from the context of God's larger purposes for life. A kids' book that my (Jenny's) daughter received for her first birthday opens with these lines: "You're here for a reason, you certainly are. The world would be different without you, by far." It goes on, "A piece of this world that is precious and dear would surely be missing if you weren't here."[1] This message that every person matters and every person has something unique to contribute to the world sounds nice—even similar to the Christian idea of individual purpose and worth. But if you read on, you'll see that this particular book's lesson—the universal purpose it promotes—is that we should spread kindness in our special way, doing "the smallest of things" to make the world a better place. But why? The book offers no answer. Why is being kind superior to being mean? Why should we make the world a better place—to what end? Divorced from a larger spiritual framework, the message is ultimately meaningless.

It is only within a framework of pursuing God's ambitions that we can truly realize our purpose, both individually and as a member of the worldwide body of Christ (in which each member has a special role). Our sense of purpose combined with the hope of eternal life serve as powerful motivators, giving deeper meaning to our activities and helping us persevere with conviction and commitment.

Of course, people who do not live by a biblical worldview still have unique gifts—innate talents for music, art, mathematical intuition, or storytelling, for example—and achieve a variety of unique feats. These distinctions still witness to the Creator even if he is not acknowledged as their source.

THREE DIMENSIONS OF PURPOSE

So, what is this larger purpose and framework? Let's zoom out and orient ourselves. Beyond an individual's unique purpose is God's universal purpose for believers. But even beyond that purpose there is a third dimension of purpose: God's ultimate purpose for everyone and everything. We can think of these three dimensions of purpose as concentric circles (visualized in fig. 7.1).[2]

✦ The larger, outer circle is God's *ultimate purpose for all people.*

✦ The second (middle) circle represents *God's universal purpose for all followers of Jesus Christ.*

✦ The third (center) circle represents the *unique purpose for which God has called each individual to himself.*

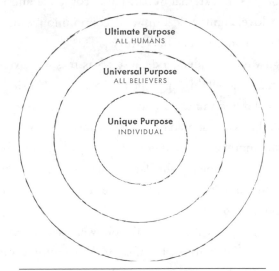

Figure 7.1. Three dimensions of purpose

Ultimate purpose. The overarching or ultimate purpose of everyone and everything is, to a degree, mysterious and unknowable by humans. Why, ultimately, did God create the universe? Why did he create humans? Why is there something rather than nothing?

We can certainly glean clues from Scripture. The Bible is clear, for example, that *everything* in the universe radiates God's glory—including human beings: moral, intelligent beings made in his image who can respond to their Maker's powers, person, and perfections with praise and wonder.[3] (Note that even those who do not tap into

this capacity and do not respond to God with praise and wonder—
that is, even his unwilling servants—ultimately serve his purposes
[cf. Genesis 50:20; Proverbs 21:1; Acts 2:23; Romans 9:22-23].) In
addition, the Bible indicates that God's ultimate aim for people is for
us to dwell in his presence forever, though not all will do so—one of
the great mysteries of life.[4] Furthermore, God created out of an expression of who he is because he wanted to, not because he was bored
or lonely. As a self-existent being outside of time, space, energy, and
matter, God has no external needs. He is complete and perfect in
himself (in love, communication, and communion with the other
persons of the Trinity) for all of eternity.

Although we can understand these ideas to some extent, much
mystery remains about this bigger picture of reality. It is simply impossible for our limited minds to grasp God's ultimate purpose for all
things. And this is as it should be. A God whose wisdom and ways we
could fully comprehend would not be worthy of our worship. At the
same time simply knowing this larger purpose exists—and having
some understanding of it—helps put the second and third layers of
God's purposes into context.

Universal purpose. All of God's followers are involved in the
second layer of God's purpose for life. There are multiple ways to sum
up this layer. "To know Christ and make him known" is one of the
most popular ways. This twofold purpose is encapsulated in one
command in the Great Commission of Matthew 28: *make disciples.*
That one command is modified by three participles—*going, baptizing,*
and *teaching*: "*Go* therefore and make disciples of all nations, *baptizing*
them in the name of the Father and of the Son and of the Holy Spirit,
teaching them to observe all that I have commanded you. And behold,
I am with you always, to the end of the age" (Matthew 28:19-20,
emphasis added).

Evangelism (*going*) leads to conversion, symbolized by baptism, but
this is not the end game. Rather, it is the gateway to edification

(*teaching*), also known as obedience-based discipleship. The cycle continues as new disciples become his agents in the world, and they too go and make disciples. Thus another way of summing up God's universal purpose for his people is "edification and evangelism." The former involves spiritual growth (increasingly coming to know God more) while the latter involves spiritual reproduction (making him known).

Let's explore this universal purpose in a bit more detail.

Knowing him. When we talk about knowing God, we're talking about experiential knowledge: knowing him as a person, not just knowing *about* him. There's an eternity's worth of difference between the two. The apostle Paul highlighted this personal knowledge when he wrote to the early believers, "I count everything as loss because of the surpassing worth of *knowing Christ Jesus* my Lord" (Philippians 3:8, emphasis added).

Knowing Christ was supreme for Paul, as it should be for every believer. And when we know him, his Spirit lives in us, and we become like him: "Those whom he foreknew he also predestined to be *conformed to the image of his Son*, in order that he might be the firstborn among many brothers" (Romans 8:29, emphasis added). Knowing Christ by placing our trust in him for forgiveness and new life sets us on a path of becoming more like Jesus—a growth process that is only complete when we join him in heaven.

Jesus himself was clear about this universal purpose. In his high priestly prayer, on the night of his betrayal and arrest in Jerusalem, Jesus prayed about his disciples coming to know the Father through himself: "This is eternal life, that they know you, the only true God, and Jesus Christ whom you have sent" (John 17:3). Again, from this verse, we see that knowing God is not merely propositional and theological but personal and devotional.

The greatest treasure a person can own is increasing intimacy with the living Lord of all creation. Although this should be our highest ambition, many believers give their hearts to the quest for lesser goods and boast and delight in things that are destined to perish. We'll avoid this trap if we heed the powerful words of Jeremiah:

> Thus says the LORD: "Let not the wise man boast in his wisdom, let not the mighty man boast in his might, let not the rich man boast in his riches, but let him who boasts boast in this, that he understands and *knows me*, that I am the LORD who practices steadfast love, justice, and righteousness in the earth. For in these things I delight, declares the LORD." (Jeremiah 9:23-24, emphasis added)

This path of knowing God involves fullness of life and joy, but it also entails identifying with Christ's sufferings and death (Philippians 3:10). As Paul says in Romans 8:28, somehow God can use "all things" in our lives—the good and bad, even death itself—to enact his plan for our lives. Although we may not ever see or fully understand how all these things are working together, we can be assured that God is working out his universal purpose, for us as individuals and for his church as a whole, to lead more and more people to know his Son and be conformed to his image.[5]

Making him known. Spiritual reproduction is the second part of our universal purpose as believers. A drive, even a necessity, to reproduce is innate to all living beings. When a person is born again and becomes a "new creature" in Christ (John 3:3-8; 2 Corinthians 5:17), this need applies. We almost instinctively want to share our newfound faith with others, with the hope that they too will come to know him. (Unfortunately, this impulse can wear off with time because of human forgetfulness and disobedience; God is always urging us to return to that state of first love.)

A precondition for reproduction is, generally speaking, health: physical health for physical reproduction and spiritual health for spiritual reproduction. The healthier we are, the more successful we will be at reproduction—and the healthier our offspring will tend to be.

We cannot give away to others what we do not ourselves possess. The more we know Christ ourselves, the easier it will be to introduce and manifest him to others. Therefore, *being in* Christ must always precede *doing for* Christ. Put another way, intimacy should animate activity, including evangelistic activity. Too often we reverse this order, hoping our activities will generate a closer relationship with God. Instead, our activities suffer. We rely less on God and may even experience burnout.

How do we make Christ known to others? First, we tell them the good news of the gospel of Christ through both verbal and nonverbal actions. The gospel is based on a set of propositions, which Paul outlines clearly: Christ died for our sins according to the Old Testament, he was buried, he was raised from the dead on the third day, and he was seen by many witnesses, including Paul himself (1 Corinthians 15:3-8).

Evangelism has multiple stages. Many of us immediately go to the final stage—the point of conversion. But stages of preevangelism (loving and serving others) are just as critical. Before the harvest come the less-glamorous steps of cultivating the soil, sowing seeds, weeding, and watering. Like farming or gardening, evangelism is a process, not a single event, and the results are ultimately up to God, not us (1 Corinthians 3:7).

When a new convert is born, spiritual reproduction isn't over; it just takes a new form—edification. Jesus commanded us to make disciples, not merely converts. Thus, conversion is only the beginning. Making Christ known also involves teaching and training. It entails modeling life in Christ for fellow believers, especially younger ones (in terms of spiritual age), by manifesting the fruit and gifts of the Spirit. We can teach, love, serve, admonish, share generously, and establish mentor-protégé relationships. In short, we can do for others what Christ did for his twelve disciples during the three years he was with them.

To summarize, God's universal purpose for the church prepares his people (that is, his disciples) for his ultimate purpose for humanity: to bring him glory and enjoy him forever (as the Westminster Shorter Catechism puts it). As we come to know God more intimately and make him known to others, we prepare to dwell with him and magnify his name for all eternity—that is, to proclaim his excellencies (1 Peter 2:9).

Unique purpose. God's unique purpose for individual Christians is the third component. This is the way a believer manifests God's universal purpose in a way that only that person can—through the unique prism of his or her personality and background.

Our unique purpose is not something we come up with out of thin air. Rather, it's given to us by God; it's not something we devise but something we discover. At the same time we often have to work to understand and articulate our purpose. For some of us this process will be more deductive, while for others it will be more revelatory (even a vision from God). For some it will look more impressive and history-making (as for the list of biblical examples at the beginning of this chapter), but we should remember that any life lived for his glory is impressive—even if it doesn't make headlines in human history.

A COMMUNITY CONTEXT

It is the responsibility of every follower of Christ to embrace both his or her unique purpose and the two-part universal purpose that unique purpose stems from—never losing sight of that larger mandate on all believers. Following Jesus is not a venture for a lone ranger. Yes, faith is personal, but it is also corporate. Our individual purposes are inextricably tied to the universal purpose of Christ's body, which is called to obey its Head, Christ himself (Colossians 1:18; 2:19).

Paul reminds us, "There is one body and one Spirit—just as also you were called in one hope that belongs to your call" (Ephesians 4:4); in this body, every single part has a role—a special place. The health and growth of the church depend on "each part . . . working properly" (Ephesians 4:16). When one part fails to do its job, the rest of the body suffers.

We should never separate ourselves from this community context when we are considering our unique purpose. Our purpose is not merely for our own fulfillment or enjoyment—it's for the building up, strengthening, and equipping of the whole body of Christ, whose members collectively reflect him and his love to the world. In other words the body gathered (edification) empowers the body scattered (evangelism).[6]

Mentoring, counseling, pastoring, coaching, (role) modeling, and friendships are often the tools God uses to help us recalibrate and to help us understand and fulfill our unique purpose. Other people can help point us to where God has gifted us, and they can also help steer us away from pursuits that don't suit us. In addition, God uses his people not just individually but collectively. Our purposes intersect and complement one another; we *can't* fulfill our individual purpose without other people. When we work in tandem, the result is greater than the sum of the parts.

This dynamic is in play in the words you're reading now. Although both of us are writers, Ken is the primary teacher and expert; I (Jenny) edit, synthesize, and build on Ken's ideas. Ken is usually the theorizer, while I'm always looking for the *so what?* for our readers. Put both of our heads together and the final product is better than if just one of us worked on this book.

RECALIBRATING

Discovering your unique purpose can be exciting and fulfilling. In this pursuit you will be most rewarded—with satisfaction that doesn't fade—when your primary aim is pleasing God (by knowing Christ and making him known).

A prophet once rebuked the foolish King Asa of Judah, saying, "The eyes of the LORD move to and fro throughout the earth that He may strongly support those whose heart is completely His" (2 Chronicles 16:9 NASB). God makes his purpose clear to those whose heart is completely his. "The LORD confides in those who fear him" (Psalm 25:14 NIV). Before asking, What's my unique purpose? we do well to dwell on the prerequisite question, Does God have all of my heart? (Is pleasing him my goal above all else?)

Commitment precedes knowledge. When we're all in, willing to risk what we need to risk of earthly possessions and status, we are ready to launch "a prayerful process of discovery that involves a thoughtful assessment of what God has gifted, called, and equipped you to do."[7]

READ AND REFLECT ON
Psalm 139 and Ephesians 2:10

Prayer: Lord, I pray that you will give me a heart that desires to know you above all else. Flowing out of my relationship with you, may I have a growing desire to make you known. As I center my mind and heart on you, please help me discern my unique role in your kingdom. Most importantly, encourage and empower me to live out that purpose. Amen.

CHAPTER SEVEN

Discovering Your Unique Purpose

I cry out to God Most High,
to God who fulfills his purpose for me.

Psalm 57:2

Some of us come to understand God's purpose for us when we're older, others when we're younger; some after a long process of discovery, others through a sudden insight or vision. For the prophet Jeremiah, the discovery came when he was a teenager:

> Before I formed you in the womb I knew you,
> and before you were born I consecrated you;
> I appointed you a prophet to the nations. (Jeremiah 1:5)

"A prophet to the nations." Can you imagine receiving such a message around age thirteen? No wonder Jeremiah responded as he did, "Ah, Lord, God! Behold, I do not know how to speak, for I am only a youth" (v. 6).

Jeremiah understood the calling (at least on a basic level), but he did not feel equipped to fulfill it. *I'm too young,* he thought.

But God would have none of Jeremiah's excuses and instead assured the young man that he would be with him every step of the way (vv. 7-8, 9-10).

Jeremiah went on to become the "weeping prophet" of the Old Testament. His life was plagued by adversity of all kinds. Ridiculed, rejected, and even thrown into the bottom of a cistern at one time (where he would have died if he hadn't been rescued), the message God sent him to deliver was not exactly popular. But neither was Jeremiah alone as he lived out his calling. God didn't call him and then turn him loose to figure things out; God was continually with him, delivering his message through his prophet and assuring him of his presence.

Still, do you wonder how often Jeremiah doubted his calling? Or wanted to run from it?

Finding our unique purpose can be fun and rewarding. It can also lead to sweat and tears, even persecution. Few stories of finding purpose in life come without some element of pain or hardship. And often the impact of pursuing our calling is largely hidden from us in this lifetime.

KEN'S PURPOSE

For me (Ken) personally, exploring and understanding my life purpose has almost always come about during times of setbacks. I tend to run ahead of the Spirit, not behind; I am always relearning the need to patiently wait for his leading and timing. It's often in the context of these setbacks and the process of recalibration they prompt that my unique purpose has been clarified, and I have come to renew my commitment to that purpose.

Sometime around the late 1990s I had been wrestling with my personal sense of purpose for about a year and a half. I had a growing collection of others' purpose statements. One day I got in the car with some friends to go to a restaurant, and on the way I suddenly saw it—my purpose came to me in a moment of convergence: *To be a lover and servant of God and others.*

This statement is visualized in table 8.1.

Table 8.1. Ken's purpose in four quadrants

	God	Others
Lover	Lover of God	Lover of others
Servant	Servant of God	Servant of others

It's important to tease out more concretely how our purpose looks in everyday life (this is partly what tool 11 is for). Whenever I assess my activities and commitments, my purpose statement serves as an overarching filter. It's a heuristic tool, helping me know when to consider pursuing an opportunity or not. (There are other factors as well, of course, including the personal counsel of the Holy Spirit.)

Notice, my purpose statement is more conceptual and internal in focus, while Jeremiah's was more functional and external in focus (being a prophet to the nations is *how* he would fulfill an inward calling to love and testify to the truth). Both statements, though, are an extension of the larger mandate to know God and make him known—directly paralleling the two Great Commandments (to love God and love others).

Whereas few people claim a calling like Jeremiah's, any believer can take my purpose statement for their own. What is unique about it is not so much the statement in and of itself but how it relates to my personality and context (see tool 11 for details). My ministry has always been focused on God first (as my primary audience) and people second. Even in my seventies, I'm greatly energized by the strong relational aspect of my vocation—my three weekly studies, myriad one-on-one discipleship and mentoring relationships, and a host of other relationships (from friends and family to colleagues and collaborators).

WHY HAVE A PURPOSE STATEMENT?

Purpose is, or should be, the beginning point of any enterprise or activity. Most CEOs of corporations and other entities appoint a committee to draft a purpose (or mission or vision) statement to reflect and guide the organization's activity. If a proposed activity or venture does not contribute to the organization's purpose vis-à-vis the purpose statement, it is (or should be) eliminated. A company's purpose statement isn't (usually) set in stone; rather, it is revisited and revised from time to time. It's a starting point, an aspiration—something to get the ship out of the dock and moving in the right direction.

Interestingly, many of the same CEOs who insist on a purpose statement for their organizations don't have a similar, carefully crafted purpose statement for their own lives, either in their minds or written down. Nor have most extrapolated their purpose to its logical impact on the many facets of their life: family, friendships, ministry and church, workplace, civic involvement, and so on.

Someone once quipped, "If you don't know where you're going, any road will take you there." Picking up on this journey metaphor again, imagine a friend telling you his family is about to set off on a two-week vacation. When you inquire about the details of the journey—travel, destination, activities—his answers are all the same: "Not sure yet; we'll decide later. We're still thinking about it." How can a person take a vacation without knowing the destination? Even if the trip is an expression of *wanderlust*, going wherever the road takes you, even *that* kind of trip has a purpose—to explore, discover, travel, experience—and thus requires some minimum-level planning.

Everything has a purpose. And just as a company does with its mission statement, we can revisit (and revise) a personal purpose statement for our lives as God shows us more of the special role he has given us in his kingdom. A purpose statement doesn't tell us every activity we should do. It's not a litmus test but a tool for assessing the opportunities that come our way. It gives us a tangible target so we won't waste time going in circles or stumbling in the dark without a defined sense of direction. It can help us avoid overcommitting or agreeing to do things we'll regret later.

How to Discover Your Purpose

The Danish philosopher and theologian Søren Kierkegaard once suggested the wisdom of defining the journey of life backward. Applying this advice means starting with your ultimate destination and working backward to your starting point (wherever you are right now). This mindset enables you to set out on any given day with confidence that your life is accomplishing the intended goals. Just as no one would set out on a vacation without a destination in mind, no one should live without a clear purpose (destination) in mind. And as long as you haven't reached your destination yet (if you're reading this, you haven't), it's never too late to begin living with this kind of intentionality on a day-to-day basis.

In *Conformed to His Image* I (Ken) wrote,

> Every believer has a unique combination of experiences, gifts, and relational networks that form a sphere of ministry opportunities. We can be assured that the Lord will not call us to a task for which he has not equipped us (1 Thessalonians 5:24), but we can also be certain that the development of our life message and purpose does not [typically] happen suddenly.[1]

Along these lines, the two most critical components in the process of discerning your unique purpose are

1. persistent prayer

2. time in the Scriptures

In terms of prayer we must remember that we don't discover the unique purpose for our lives on our own, apart from the Purpose Giver. Rather,

This is a divine-human process of preparation and illumination in which each of our positive and negative experiences can be sovereignly used by God in such a way that we can, through his power, make a lasting impact in the lives of others. . . . We must trust God enough to commit ourselves in advance to whatever he calls us to be and to do.[2]

In addition to prayer God uses our time in the Scriptures to train and equip us for ministry. We must get past shallow Bible reading (including cherry-picking verses out of their context) and dependence on others (through devotionals and commentaries). The deeper our study, the more of his Word we hide away in our hearts and minds, the deeper our knowledge of God and his will for us.

Besides the two essential components of prayer and time in God's Word, we do well to identify or review our

+ experiences and background
+ natural gifts or proclivities
+ education and other training and skills
+ temperament and personality
+ roles and relationships
+ spiritual gifts

Finally, we need others. In fact, without wise people speaking into our lives—noticing and telling us, "Yes, this is you" or "No, that's not your strength"—it is often hard for us to be objective in identifying the things just listed.

Each of these components of our lives is relevant to the specific outworking of God's purpose in and through us. Our unique purpose is rarely revealed in a moment and may take time and discipline to discover. It may be manifested in different (or expanding) ways across the seasons of life. Regardless, it's well worth the effort to understand our unique role in God's kingdom. If we don't identify our purpose with conviction, we'll pick it up by imitation or default. We and the church will be better off if we pursue it intentionally, with a mindset of stewardship (the topic of section three).

UNIQUE PURPOSE IN THE BIBLE

The Bible is replete with examples and references that point to the existence of this unique purpose for each person. Christianity is unique among the world religions in its attention to individuals—*every* individual, from any station of life and any epoch. Whether a person is a king or a commoner, a social elite or an outcast, each person has dignity and purpose in God's eyes.

Jesus Christ. One has to wonder, did Jesus' earthly parents tell him about the details of his birth—that he was conceived by the Holy Spirit, that his name meant "the Lord saves," that he was the fulfillment of the Immanuel prophecy in Isaiah 7:14, that he would save his people from their sins (Matthew 1:20-25)? We can't answer these questions with certainty. But from his words to his parents as a twelve-year-old at the temple in Jerusalem—"Did you not know that I must be in my Father's house?" (Luke 2:49)—it's clear Jesus had some idea, even as a youth, of the purposeful calling on his life. Likely, he grew into his understanding of that calling, given that Luke also tells us that Jesus "increased in wisdom" over time (Luke 2:52). And this realization of purpose no doubt occurred, as it does for us, through intimacy with his Father in prayer.

By the time he began his public ministry in his early thirties, Jesus was quite aware of his purpose. His most succinct summaries of that purpose include the following:

✦ "Even the Son of Man came not to be served but to serve, and to give his life as a ransom for many" (Mark 10:45).

✦ "The Son of Man came to seek and to save the lost" (Luke 19:10).

✦ "For this purpose I was born and for this purpose I came into the world—to bear witness to the truth" (John 18:37).

Perfect as he was, Jesus never strayed from his unique purpose on earth—never doubted, never deviated from what God was revealing to him. He might have had a variety of names (such as Suffering Servant, Prince of Peace, Son of Man), but everything he did revolved around his singular purpose of glorifying his Father by seeking, serving, and saving lost people, and by testifying to the truth.

Even still, a lifetime of guidance was needed for Jesus to understand and live his purpose. We can learn from his example, regularly seeking God's direction and wisdom, and remaining open (no matter how old and experienced we are) to new ways God wants to fulfill his purpose for us.[3]

The apostle Paul. The apostle Paul had the unusual advantage of both converting to Christianity and receiving his unique purpose as a (new) follower of Christ in a matter of just a few days. Christ first appeared to Paul (also known as Saul) on the road to Damascus in dramatic fashion. He then led Paul to the house of a man named Ananias, who God used to reveal the unique part Paul would play in the establishment and growth of the early church.

Three days after Paul encountered the risen Christ, "The Lord said to [Ananias], 'Go, for [Saul/Paul] is a chosen instrument of mine to carry my name before the Gentiles and kings and the children of Israel'" (Acts 9:15; see also Acts 22:6-21; 26:12-18).

Paul's purpose was an extension of believers' larger mandate to edify and evangelize, to know and please Christ. From verses such as Romans 11:13, 1 Timothy 2:7, and 2 Timothy 1:11, it's clear that Paul was keenly aware of his unique calling to be an apostle to and a teacher of the Gentiles. And how did the apostle to the Gentiles gain specific direction for fulfilling this unique purpose? The same way Jesus did (and the same way we do): by devoting his life to knowing God, communicating with the Lord regularly in prayer, and then obeying what was revealed to him. (Philippians 3:7-11, Galatians 1:10, and 2 Corinthians 5:9 offer further glimpses into Paul's heart to please the Lord and be faithful to his calling.)

The woman with the alabaster flask. It's not too hard to believe that God had a unique purpose for Jesus or people like Paul or Jeremiah. But consider the anonymous woman who anointed Jesus with very expensive perfume shortly before his death and burial.

> While [Jesus] was at Bethany in the house of Simon the leper, as he was reclining at table, a woman came with an alabaster flask of ointment of pure nard, very costly, and she broke the flask and poured it over his head. There were some who said to themselves indignantly, "Why was the ointment wasted like that? For this ointment could have been sold for more than three hundred denarii and given to the poor." And they scolded her. But Jesus said, "Leave her alone. Why do you trouble her? She has done a beautiful thing to me. . . . And truly, I say to you, wherever the gospel is proclaimed in the whole world, what she has done will be told in memory of her." (Mark 14:3-6, 9)

This woman's extravagant worship of and love for Jesus was an expression (in part) of her unique role in God's kingdom. And although we don't know her name, her example edifies believers and testifies to Jesus' identity to this day. Her story is a great illustration of the fact that we don't have to be world-famous or to be on a mission to do great things for God for him to use us.

He can use the simplicity of our faithfulness, in the singular context of our lives and personalities, to achieve his higher purposes.

JENNY'S UNIQUE PURPOSE

In contrast to Ken, I (Jenny) am still coming to a clearer understanding and articulation of my unique purpose through a more deductive process. At forty-one, I have seen enough patterns in my life to have a sense of how God seems to use me. But my own purpose statement has an "under construction" sign on it still: *To embrace and reflect, with excellence, the truth, goodness, and beauty of God.*

The two verbs capture the universal purpose of every believer: knowing Christ (*embrace*) and making Christ known (*reflect*). Each of the four other keywords has particular meaning for me, and each one is lived in my current roles as an editor, writer, apologetics conference director, photographer and artist, mother, wife, daughter, and friend. I resonate with the three transcendentals (truth, goodness, and beauty) in specific, personal ways, and the idea of excellence reflects my innate drive (which I've had my entire conscious life) to do all things well— not for my own glory but as a reflection of the Creator.

My sense of purpose is still unfolding, especially as I navigate the transition from being a full-time work-from-home editor and writer to being a full-time stay-at-home mother. I already see parallels between these two stages, however. As one example, I have been creating greeting cards with my photography for most of my adult life— intending to call people's attention to the beauty of the created order (while filling the inside with words of truth and gratitude). I also use my nature photography in my paid work. Now, I often call my daughter's attention to the beauty of God's creation during leisurely walks in our neighborhood. This comes naturally to me, as does quoting a verse or two from a psalm to point her beyond the creation to the Creator. What a delight it is when I now hear Heidi spontaneously exclaiming back to me, "Look at those pretty flowers, Mom!"

RECALIBRATING

A mistake we can make in pursuing our purpose is to become so caught up in assessing and fulfilling ourselves that we lose sight of the bigger picture, the larger purpose God has for his church as a whole. One of the most helpful things you can do to understand your purpose is to talk to other people. Talk to those who know you well and to those who know you in different contexts. Ask them, If you could sum me up in a sentence, what would you say? It takes humility and openness to do this. But it can be very valuable because others can assess our strengths better than we can, and they may also see blind spots we can't. When we're uncertain, sometimes others can draw us out (Proverbs 20:5).

The paralysis of analysis sometimes prevents us from acting, but any CEO will attest to the fact that a half-baked purpose statement is better for a company than no statement at all. The same is true for an individual. *You can always revise it!* You can also try a statement on for size (say, for a week or month) to see if it seems to fit or capture you. If not, go back to the dressing room and try another one. (This works, of course, as long as your statement stays tethered to God's universal purpose for believers.)

With a purpose statement in hand and a heart that relies on God and his grace, you're ready to explore in more concrete ways how God wants you to invest all that he has given you. We'll explore that topic in part three.

. . . .
READ AND REFLECT ON
Luke 19:10 and John 17:4
. . . .

Prayer: Lord, thank you that you have given me a unique role and purpose among your followers, with the larger goal of knowing you and making you known. Please help me discern and live out the unique purpose that you have for me so that I may ultimately bring glory to your name on earth and in heaven. Amen.

TOOL 11: PROCESSING YOUR UNIQUE PURPOSE

Jesus wants us to have the incredible aliveness of doing something wonderful with our lives.[4] Most of what we do won't amount to a hill of beans before God. Our credentials won't matter much at the

Judgment Seat. We are all going to die one day. What do we want to have lived for? When we know that, we can begin to prayerfully develop our purpose (or mission) statement.

Seek clarity for your vision of purpose. Don't increase your activities, but through prayer, exposure to Scripture, and times of reflection ask God for discernment. This process may take weeks, months, or even years.

Write a brief (one sentence, if possible) statement of purpose that defines why you think God has put you on this earth. This statement should aim to encapsulate your *unchanging reason for being* and hold true regardless of your life circumstances. A few examples are at the end of this tool.

Note: We have talked to couples who have developed purpose statements for their marriages and families. You can certainly adapt this tool for that purpose.

Employ your concise purpose statement to determine and evaluate your objectives and activities. What goals follow from the purpose you've defined?

Prayerfully reflect on your global and role purposes (see example at the end of this tool).

Next, consider what specific goals and objectives would assist you in fulfilling these purposes for your life.

Review your purpose statement and goals regularly (at least annually), refining them as God gives you greater clarity regarding your purpose. The key is to examine your activities in light of your purpose rather than the other way around. In this way your life will be determined more by the Word than by the external pressures of the world.

Strive to live by your purpose statement every day, and notice how much it (and your list of specific goals) helps keep your life on track. You may be amazed how much a Christ-centered purpose brings harmony to all areas of your life (family, work, finances, ministry, etc.).

Example: Here is my (Ken's) own purpose statement, along with the global and unique role purposes that flow from it.

My personal purpose statement: To be a lover and servant of God and others.

To fulfill my purpose as a lover and servant of God and others, three global purposes follow from Scripture:

Global purpose 1. Love God completely—know God and his character and grow into the image of his Son in faith, hope, and love.

Global purpose 2. Love myself correctly—see myself in the light of God's character and grow in humility and obedience.

Global purpose 3. Love others compassionately—see others in the light of God's character and grow in love and service.

From these global purposes, I determined seven role purposes for my own life:

Role purpose 1. Husband—love and serve my wife and help her live up to her full potential.

Role purpose 2. Father—love and serve my daughter and son-in-law in such a way that they know their parents love God.

Role purpose 3. Son—love and serve my mother and father, to let them know they are honored and cherished. (I wrote this while my parents were living.)

Role purpose 4. Friend—love and serve my friends through commitment, transparency, and vulnerability in relationships of mutual acceptance and esteem.

Role purpose 5. Neighbor—love and serve my neighbors in such a way that they want to know Christ or grow in him.

Role purpose 6. Minister—love and serve unbelievers and believers in such a way that believers are edified and unbelievers are evangelized.

Role purpose 7. Writer and publisher—love and serve readers in a way that helps them manifest eternal values in a temporal arena, drawing them into intimacy with God and better understanding the culture they live in.

Sample Purpose Statements (Can Be Adapted for Personal Use)

Scripture-based

✦ to have the mind of Christ in everything (1 Corinthians 2:16)

✦ to lose my life for his sake (Mark 8:35)

✦ to count everything as loss because of the surpassing worth of knowing Christ, or to count everything else as rubbish that I may gain Christ (Philippians 3:8)

✦ to live to serve rather than to be served (Matthew 20:28; Mark 10:45)

✦ to be poured out as a drink offering in sacrificial service to God and others (Philippians 2:7; 2 Timothy 4:6)

✦ to seek the approval of God, not of humans (Galatians 1:10)

✦ to trust the Father, abide in the Son, and walk by the Spirit (John 14:1; 15:4; Galatians 5:16)

✦ to live as a sojourner and exile on earth, with reverent fear (1 Peter 2:11)

✦ to proclaim the excellences of him who called you out of darkness into his marvelous light (1 Peter 2:9)

Based on extrabiblical sources

✦ to spend the rest of my earthly life for the will of God (Patrick Morley)

✦ find out what the Holy Spirit is doing, and then get on it (Robert A. Cook)

✦ find out where God is at work and join him there (Henry Blackaby)

✦ to be a sign and an agent of the love of Christ (Joe Ehrmann)

✦ exalt and internalize God's truth and reflect that truth to others (Kevin Murray)

✦ to hear and help other men hear "Well done" in this life and the next (John Bishop)

✦ to be a man or woman after God's own heart in every area of life (Anonymous)

PART III

PRACTICE

How Do I Wisely
Invest My Life?

CHAPTER EIGHT

STEWARDING ALL THAT GOD GIVES

As each one has received a special gift,
employing it in serving one another as good stewards
of the manifold grace of God.

1 PETER 4:10 NASB

I am a great sinner, but Christ is a great Savior."[1] These were some of the final words of John Newton and a great summary of the life purpose of the famed preacher, hymn writer, author, and church leader. To put it even more succinctly, Newton—after his well-known conversion to Christ—was all about *amazing grace* (the title of his most famous hymn).

Newton, a former slave trader, initially turned to Christ during a storm on the high seas of the mid-Atlantic in 1748. He later agonized over his vocation, even writing a thorough self-examination of the process. After he discerned his calling to the pastorate at age thirty-three, Newton suffered "six years of frustrations, disappointments, and rejections."[2] Yet, he eventually went on to become a "patriarchal figure in the evangelical movement."[3]

Biographer Jonathan Aitken chronicles multiple transitions in Newton's life following his dramatic conversion, each marked by various challenges. He notes that, as influential as Newton's pastoring, hymn and book writing, and church leadership were, one of his greatest contributions to history, humanity, and God's kingdom was his mentorship of William Wilberforce. "Newton was a spiritual sage, but he also had secular wisdom," Aitken writes. "It was this combination that enabled him to rise to the greatest challenge of his later years—influencing William Wilberforce and supporting his campaign to abolish the slave trade."[4] Wilberforce was on the verge of quitting his political career when Newton stepped in as a mentor and supporter. Without Wilberforce, and thus without Newton, the African slave trade would not have been abolished when it was.

Wilberforce was far from the only person Newton invested in. Newton, who was married but never had children of his own, encouraged and advised countless young clergy, missionaries, and others (some went on to become noted leaders themselves, like William Cowper and William Carey). Fueling Newton's investment in people was his deep relationship with and commitment to God. A true steward of the "manifold grace of God" (1 Peter 4:10 NASB), Newton (because of his past) had a keen sense of his unworthiness as a sinner side by side with an "overflowing thankfulness . . . to God."[5] As a result, he became an effective proclaimer and channel of God's grace in everything he did.

STEWARDS OF GRACE

On our earthly sojourns we are called in Christ to wisely invest our lives—all that God gives us—in such a way that we fulfill his purpose for us and arrive at our eternal home to the words, "Well done, good and faithful servant" (Matthew 25:23). Another term for this responsibility is *stewardship*.

A steward is charged with investing or managing the possessions of another. Biblical stewardship is about far more than money or even tangible possessions. It's about recognizing and living in light of the fact that everything we have and are come from God, even our bodies, and all is to be returned to him in the form of faithful service (1 Corinthians 6:20). *Everything.* This includes God's mercy and grace, which he has freely given, and which he asks us to freely extend to others (Matthew 6:12; Luke 6:36; 1 Peter 4:10). This was what John Newton did so well.

Stewarding our lives and possessions well is central to living with an eternal perspective because it reflects our understanding that nothing we have is ultimately ours (1 Chronicles 29:14). We invest our lives in part—our talents, time, and other resources—by staying true to our calling rather than getting sidetracked by other pursuits.

FIVE AREAS OF STEWARDSHIP

In this section we will examine five critical areas of stewardship: time, talent, treasure (finances), truth, and relationships. We have touched on these areas in various ways already, but here our focus is on the practical and the actionable. When we're recalibrating, it's often one or more of these five areas that need some adjustment.

For example, we may be experiencing a relational crisis that requires a change in how we are stewarding both our time and relationships. Or we may be in a work-related transition that requires reexamining how we're using our talent and finances so we can better understand how to pursue a job that will honor how God uniquely wired us while also meeting our income needs. Or maybe we are facing retirement, and God has given us great wisdom and spiritual knowledge; we want to know how to invest the truth he has revealed to us so that we become generational links in his kingdom and don't squander this unique season of life.

Earlier in life, we tend to have a little of each of these five resources (and may be impatient for more of all of them, especially treasure). As people age they tend to see increases in four of the five resources that

God gives—talent, treasure, truth, and relationships—even as the fifth (time) is dwindling. Of course, this is not always the case (some continue to experience tight finances to the end of their lives). Good stewards focus on glorifying their Owner to the very end of life, no matter how much or little of each resource we have.

THE MANTLE OF STEWARDSHIP

Human beings were created to be stewards of God's creation. God is the owner of all that exists; we are merely managers on his behalf, investing that which he ultimately owns but entrusts to us temporarily, on his behalf.

The planet's first stewards, Adam and Eve, received these instructions: "Be fruitful and multiply and fill the earth and subdue it, and have dominion over the fish of the sea and over the birds of the heavens and over every living thing that moves on the earth" (Genesis 1:28). The first couple was also commanded to "work [the garden of Eden] and keep it" (Genesis 2:15); to eat any of the plants (Genesis 1:29) and trees except one, the tree of the knowledge of good and evil (Genesis 2:17); and to name the animals (Genesis 2:19). Adam was furthermore commanded to leave his parents and "hold fast to his wife" in a new, one-flesh relationship (Genesis 2:24). So humans stood in the middle, between God and his creation, with their stewardship charge encompassing not only physical resources but also time, work, knowledge, and relationships.

Not all humans have embraced this original, God-given stewardship responsibility, of course. But all who have been reconciled to God through Jesus Christ take that mantle upon themselves. We're called to live with the mindset expressed by Paul in 1 Corinthians 4:7: "What do you have that you did not receive?"

THREE CHARACTERISTICS OF GODLY STEWARDS

The biblical figures Joseph, Jesus, and Paul lived with this same mindset—focused on stewarding all that they had received from God.

These men exemplified three key characteristics of godly investment or stewardship: competence, consistency, and commitment.

When Joseph was sold into slavery in Egypt by his older brothers, his character and gifts caught the attention of Potiphar, an official of the Pharaoh. Potiphar put Joseph in charge of everything he owned. He trusted Joseph to manage everything, concerning himself with nothing except showing up for meals (Genesis 39:6)! Joseph had his head on a swivel: repeatedly turning toward Potiphar, then implementing what Potiphar expected. Joseph was a *competent* steward, and he doubtless saw his stewardship of Potiphar's belongings as an extension of his stewardship for God—who provided this position for Joseph to work in.

Jesus came to earth not to do his will but the will of the One who sent him (John 6:38). He spoke only what the Father told him to say (John 12:50), did exactly as God instructed him (John 14:31), and accomplished the work the Father gave him to do (John 17:4). Jesus was a true and perfect steward; we might describe him as a *consistent* steward—for he always undertook activities that would bring his Father pleasure and glory.

Finally, the apostle Paul modeled being a *committed* steward. Four times Paul referred to himself as a steward of God—specifically, a steward of the "mysteries" and "grace" of God (1 Corinthians 4:1; 9:17; Ephesians 3:2; Colossians 1:25). So compelling was this charge that he laid aside all competing priorities to focus solely on being faithful to his stewardship assignment (Philippians 3:7-14). In doing so he illustrated the chief trait of a steward: faithfulness or trustworthiness (1 Corinthians 4:2), which derives from commitment.

For *competent*, think *wise*. For *consistent*, think *single-minded*. For *committed*, think *faithful*. These are the traits of a godly steward. They're also the characteristics of someone who lives and finishes well, leaving a godly legacy for generations to come.

RECALIBRATING

The central question of stewardship is whether we're here on our business or God's. Is he Lord of my life, or am I? Is it *"Thy* will be done" (Matthew 6:10) or *"my* will be done" (Isaiah 14:13-14)? Will we live for ourselves or for the Lord (2 Corinthians 5:15)?

Keeping an eternal perspective on all that God gives us means always remembering that at the end of the day it all goes back in the box. We can't take anything tangible with us when we die. The physical results of our labor may disappear, but the eternal fruit will remain. Consequently, we will do well to constantly recalibrate and ask, How can I invest all God has given me—his grace, his truth, his wealth, and so on—in a way that yields eternal dividends? We'll explore the answer to that question for each of the five main areas of stewardship in the coming chapters.

. . . .

READ AND REFLECT ON
1 Corinthians 4:1-2

. . . .

Prayer: Lord, I pray that you would impress upon me the fact that all I have belongs to you. Please help me to be a competent, consistent, and committed steward—that I may honor you with how I handle your possessions. May I realize that even the grace you have shown me is something to be stewarded and given to others. Amen.

CHAPTER NINE

STEWARDING TIME

*Therefore be careful how you walk, not as unwise men
but as wise, making the most of your time,
because the days are evil.*

EPHESIANS 5:15-16 NASB

When I (Ken) was asked to preach in a historic church in Connecticut, it was like stepping back in time. The church was founded in the late 1700s; its interior bore the marks of New England Puritan influence throughout. To access the pulpit the speaker climbed a flight of stairs that put him some fifteen feet above the congregation. Suspended over the ornate pulpit was a sacred canopy—literally, an ornate wooden canopy that served to amplify the speaker's voice in the days before microphones and speakers.

When it was time for me to preach, I climbed the narrow stairs to the pulpit, a massive three-sided affair. There was a lectern in front for both Bible and notes along with a narrow, flat shelf that ran around both sides of the pulpit. I noticed two objects, one on each corner of the flat shelf. On the right of the lectern was a tall candle in an antique holder, and on the left was an antique hourglass—the sand had accumulated in the bottom well of the glass.

Suddenly it hit me—the purpose of the candle and the hourglass. In Puritan New England these objects were classic illustrations of the Latin phrase *memento mori*, which means, "Remember you're going to die." They were reminders that death is the inevitable conclusion to life—visual representations of the brief, transitory nature of this passing world. For the nonspiritual, *memento mori* might have reminded a person to "eat, drink, and be merry, for tomorrow you die." But for the follower of Jesus, *memento mori* had deeper implications: judgment is coming, redeem the time, walk circumspectly. Just as a candle burns down and its flame sputters out, and the sand runs through the hourglass, so our earthly life will come to an end—at a time known only to God.

That candle and hourglass were sobering reminders, and I wondered if the church members, who had stared up at the pulpit and those objects hundreds of times, had any idea what they were for. That day I decided if I was ever invited to preach again at that church, I knew what my Scripture text and message would be.

Two years later I was invited again to speak in that same church. And I came prepared with a message on Moses' words in Psalm 90:12:

Teach us to number our days
    that we may get a heart of wisdom.

I climbed the stairs and entered the pulpit and, without a word to the congregation, lit the candle with the matches I had brought. Then, I reached over and inverted the hourglass so the sand began draining into the bottom well. I am fairly sure this was the first time that candle and hourglass had been employed by a contemporary preacher.

When I arrived at my exposition of verse 12, I explained *memento mori* to the congregation—and the purpose of the two objects on either side of the lectern. What I was explaining was the importance of the stewardship of time—the essence of which is captured in the words, "Teach us to number our days." I explained how important it is to realize that our time is not ours but God's, and how the wise way of investing the days God gives us is by embracing the *precious present* (since, after all, we are not guaranteed the future).

At the end of the sermon I leaned over and blew out the candle. Then I took the hourglass and, instead of flipping it over, I laid it on its side and said to the congregation, "Time out." As I descended the stairs, the congregation broke out in applause. Perhaps it was, in part, a "thank you for explaining why there are a candle and hourglass on the pulpit!" But hopefully it was, in larger part, because they grasped the truth—as sobering as it was—that I was trying to communicate: Our time is short, no amount of it is guaranteed, and it is not ultimately ours; therefore, don't squander it.

MAKING THE MOST OF TIME

A less moribund way to think of the stewardship of time is found in Paul's words in Ephesians 5:15-16 (NASB): "Be careful how you walk, not as unwise men but as wise, making the most of your time, because the days are evil."

We hear a lot about time management. But a standard joke among seminar speakers is, "Nobody manages time!" And it's true. Time marches on; it cannot be stopped or started; it cannot be added to or subtracted from. No one can truly manage time. But we can *steward* the time we are given—making the most of it (some translations say "redeeming it"), as Paul says, seeing it as a gift from God.[1] Of course, the older we get, the more cognizant we tend to become that life is comparatively brief, and time is precious.

Not one of us knows how long our lives will be. Thus, it is wise for us never to presume upon the future. We make a serious mistake if, while young or even in our middle years, we assume our candle is long and our hourglass has abundant sand. This error usually shows up in the way we spend our days—devoting far more time to temporal activities (that have little eternal consequence) than we would if we knew we only had a year to live (hence tool 3). Some of us are more prone to procrastinate or get distracted, while others of us are prone to overwork or become overcommitted. Both ends of the spectrum display shortcomings in the area of stewarding time.

The reality is that each of us has exactly the amount of time God has allocated for us to accomplish his purpose for us on earth (Psalm 139:16). We do not need to fret or presumptuously dawdle when thinking about the length of our lives. Jesus lived until his early thirties and accomplished all that he was called to do; Moses lived to 120 and completed the mission God gave him as well. Knowing that God gives each of us the time we need—not one hour more or less—naturally shifts our focus from seeing time in terms of numbers (days and years, or *chronos* time) to seeing time in terms of opportunities (the content we fill those days and years with, or *kairos* time).

STEWARDING OPPORTUNITIES

There is considerable agreement that the eighteenth-century writer Samuel Johnson was the most widely accomplished man of letters in English history. His friend and biographer, James Boswell, wrote *The Life of Samuel Johnson* (1791), considered to be the finest biography in the English language. Boswell was the oldest son of a strict, aloof Scottish judge. As a child the younger Boswell relished the rare attention shown to him by his father. A story is often told of James, who, as an adult, spoke about a special day his father took him fishing, remembering what they talked about and what he learned. It was a day he never forgot, marking him for the rest of his life. However, when Judge Boswell died and his own journals and papers were being organized, someone checked his diary to see what he recorded on that day of fishing that had meant so much to his young son. The diary entry for that date contained one line: "Gone fishing with my son; a day wasted."

That sad account illustrates the two different concepts of time, *kairos* and *chronos*.

We can't control clock time (chronos), but we can seize every opportunity (kairos time) to do what the Owner of clock time desires.

James Boswell's father was focused only on *chronos*, defining a productive day by worldly standards; he totally missed the importance of *kairos*, the opportunity to be with his son. James, on the other hand, probably lost track of *chronos* as he reveled in the *kairos* of being with his father.

Kairos moments cannot be measured or planned. They can occur over a short period (in a brief encounter at a store or on the street, for example) or as a season of our lives (for example, a time when you're placed under a particular boss with whom God is clearly using you to share and model the gospel). *Kairos* opportunities are events that God orchestrates, often sovereignly putting you together with a certain person in the right place at the right time (*chronos*). We probably receive several *kairos* opportunities per day, but many of us steamroll past them due to busyness, or we're blind to them because we are not tuned in to the priorities and heart of God. This is partly why recalibrating regularly (even weekly or monthly) is so valuable.

As we get older we may feel time is slipping through our fingers, that we don't have enough time left (in terms of our calendar or our opportunities) to make much difference or to accomplish what we hoped. But what if God wants us to embrace *kairos* opportunities now, whatever state we're in, not dwelling on the past (resting on past accomplishments) or worrying about what we will or will not have time for in the future?

EXAMPLES TO FOLLOW, FROM JESUS TO TODAY

Jesus himself was known to stop everything he was doing to focus on a single person, even on what may have been viewed as a

ministry-filled, busy day. Whether it was a sick person crying out for
healing or a spiritually thirsty woman drawing water from a well, we
can be sure that Jesus never once missed a *kairos* opportunity. He who
holds the galaxies together was always on the lookout for how his
Father wanted to use him at any moment. He would halt his activities
and reduce his whole world to just one person in need. That person
became his agenda.

Investing our time wisely has much to do with the priority God
places on people and relationships. (Indeed, all areas of biblical stewardship are interconnected in some way.) We should never defer to the
future what we can and should do now, especially since there may be
no *later*.

Barry, a grandfather in his early seventies, offers a contrasting example to James Boswell's father. A practicing lawyer for nearly five
decades, Barry gradually transitioned into retirement. In 2020, about
three years into full retirement, he wrote, "I am finding that it is satisfying to work and live at a slower pace and to disengage from finding
meaning in business-level productivity; now I am gaining more appreciation and satisfaction in doing the routine affairs of life, which in
the past were great interruptions and heavy burdens." Still, Barry—
who spent years in a profession where "time is money," with every
minute accounted for and billed to the client—has to intentionally
remind himself of God's view on how he spends his time.

> This comes to mind when I have been playing hide-and-seek for
> fifteen minutes with our granddaughter, and it is about to drive
> me crazy, but she wants to keep at it; I stop and think, so what's
> the most important way for me to spend the next few minutes?
> Keep doing this or get frustrated that it's not "productive"?

Wisely investing our time means we will sometimes spend time
doing things (e.g., fishing or playing hide-and-seek) that *seem* small
and insignificant, like a waste. Stewarding time also means sacrifice (of

whatever we could be doing instead). One thing is sure, though, when we see our time as God's and treat it accordingly, we will fill our days with those things that he wants us to—prioritizing what he prioritizes. And that is a course of action that ends in one day hearing those blessed words, "Well done."

RECALIBRATING

The longer we live, the shorter our candle gets, and the less sand is left at the top of our hourglass. None of us knows how much time— *chronos* or *kairos*—we have left. Neither can we ever gain back the times now in the past.

As stewards of the time God gives us, we will be reviewed at the Judgment Seat of Christ in terms of our faithfulness, the chief trait of a steward (1 Corinthians 3:10-15; 4:2). At that time we will be accountable for our

+ *Chronos* time: the 24 hours per day, 168 hours per week, 8,760 hours per (nonleap) year, and so on, in each of our lives.

+ *Kairos* time: the opportunities when we face a choice, *How do I honor God, the Owner of time and author of history, at this moment?*

God guides and speaks to us, but he does not micromanage us. He sets our agenda and provides us with resources, but then he gives us much leeway in our stewardship role (within the boundaries of his standards). The call to "number our days" from Psalm 90 isn't a call to frenetic activity. It's a call to the intentional planning of our activities.

Remember Phil Burgess (chap. 6), whose calendar was chockful after just a few months of retirement? Whether we're twenty-five or sixty-five, there's a danger of overcommitting and of, more generally, stewarding our time poorly. Recalibration helps us take stock of our calendars and ask God how *he* wants to fill them.

· · · · · · · · · · · · · ·
READ AND REFLECT ON
Ephesians 5:14-16
· · · · · · · · · · · · · ·

Prayer: Father, teach me to live with two days in my calendar: today and *that* Day. May I be open to your promptings, not insisting on my own agenda but following your lead in how I spend the time you have given me. May I define a productive day by your standards rather than by the world's metrics. Amen.

TOOL 12: BRIEF TIPS FOR STEWARDING YOUR TIME

1. Look for *kairos* opportunities every day.

2. Minimize distractions (especially social media and phone use—don't let yourself get sucked in for hours on end; for a reality check, use an app that reports your daily smartphone use).

3. Plan the important (e.g., time with God, time with family, time with other people, time serving, personal reflection time) so it isn't always overwhelmed by the urgent (i.e., tasks that clamor to be done immediately).

4. Establish a healthy rhythm of rest and work—evaluating this balance regularly (tool 9 may help).

5. Don't skip prayer, Bible reading and study, and fellowship with the body of Christ (see them as essential).

6. Invite input from those who know you best. (Consider asking your spouse or closest relative to rate you from 1 to 10, with 1 being a poor steward of time and 10 being an excellent steward of time. Ask the person where they see room for improvement—they may be able to identify time wasters in your life better than you can.)

7. While younger and still working, don't overwork or over-commit—learn to say no, realizing the good is the enemy of the

best. (Countless people regret not spending more time with their kids when they were younger; avoid this regret before it's too late!)

8. When older and retired (or semi-retired), establish a daily routine for yourself. Many retired people find even the most general structure helpful. Examples of categories of activities to include are (1) time with God (Bible study and prayer), (2) time with others (include family/spouse and friends), (3) ministry investment and mentoring, (4) personal infrastructure/ administrative tasks, (5) health and physical well-being (e.g., a daily walk or session of stretches), (6) leisure and relaxation, and (7) any other activity you do with regularity.

Personal Reflection

✦ Reflecting on the previous tips, which *one* do you think you need to focus on applying first? What step(s) will you take to do so?

✦ What other tips do you need to work on applying? What step(s) will you take toward doing so?

CHAPTER TEN

STEWARDING TALENT

All things come from you,
and of your own have we given you.

1 CHRONICLES 29:14

Just shy of her fiftieth birthday, Julia Woodman, an army wife and homemaker, went back to school. Her husband had recently retired, and her youngest daughter had entered college. During this time of transition she looked down her own path, searching for the next step to take, when she had an epiphany during a retreat at a Benedictine monastery in Oregon. A monk there encouraged her in what she worried was a "harebrained idea," saying, "How do you know that God has not put that [idea of going back to art school] on your heart? God has created you with a sound mind, and one of the ways he trains people is through artists."[1]

The rest is history. Julia, now in her eighties, became a master silversmith who "integrate[s] spiritual devotion into her pursuit of artistry."[2] Her work has won multiple awards and is featured in collections throughout the United States as well as abroad.

Julia's late-career start in metalwork wasn't out of the blue. She was exposed to industrial design earlier in life at the Pratt Institute, specifically a principle of "synthesizing beauty and utility," and was thus aware of her inclination toward sculpting.[3] But it wasn't until she was seeking her MFA—at an age when many are thinking about winding *down* their careers—that she realized her talent in silversmithing.

"All of my success," Julia is careful to highlight, "has to do with the power of prayer."[4] Crafting each piece to the glory of God, Julia seeks inspiration from God and his Word. A cross she made for a cathedral in Atlanta, for example, was "inspired by the imagery of Psalm 19: 'God's word is sweeter than honey, even the honey that drips from the comb.' Comprised of a series of gold comblike shapes, the cross vividly evokes nectar with a spiritual aura."[5] Julia has no plans to retire as long as she's physically able to do what she loves to do, is specially skilled to do, and (she quips) "keeps [her] off the streets."[6]

Julia's story is a beautiful example of an ordinary person finding her extraordinarily unique purpose throughout a lifetime, on God's timetable. She is also a wonderful model of someone who is stewarding her talent well. Note that for her, silversmithing is a combination of innate skill (a knack wired into her by God) and training; spiritually speaking, she can use this skill to produce something that points to the Creator God, or she could use it to point back to herself or to something else in the creation. Thankfully, she has chosen to glorify God with it.

WHAT HAVE WE BEEN GIVEN?

First Chronicles 29:14 says, "All things come from you, and of your own have we given you." This verse points to the wide scope of our stewardship before God. "All things" come from God—and we owe them all back to him. These things encompass not only our material wealth and belongings but also intangible gifts—including our skills and talents, both developed and undeveloped ones, innate and acquired. For the use of all these we are accountable to the One who gives them. From what he has given us, we give back to him by investing them (on his behalf) for his purposes.

The apostle Paul echoes this idea in a verse we've seen before: "Who regards you as superior? What do you have that you did not receive? And if you did receive it, why do you boast as if you had not received it?" (1 Corinthians 4:7 NASB). The context of these words is important. There was "jealousy and strife" among the Corinthian believers; divisions had arisen over allegiances to certain leaders. Some followed Apollos, some followed Paul, some followed others. Most likely these allegiances were focused on the talents of certain leaders—their teachings, their styles, their charisma, or other traits. But Paul shut down such reasoning by reminding them that no one possesses gifts that did not come from God. In that sense all leaders are equal as servants (or stewards) of God who have been gifted to accomplish different things for him: "I planted, Apollos watered, but God gave the growth" (1 Corinthians 3:6).

When God bestows gifts and roles, there's no room for boasting or bragging. There's only room for faithfulness—wisely investing the talents God has given. "It is required of stewards that they be found faithful" (1 Corinthians 4:2).

WHAT CAN WE GIVE?

To faithfully invest our talents and abilities, we first need to *know* them. Identifying our gifts is a lifelong task, and they may change (or the way we use them may change) across the seasons of our lives. Julia Woodman had hints of her silver-crafting gift earlier, but she didn't truly become aware of and nurture it until midlife.

We can think of talent in two realms: natural abilities and spiritual abilities. Of course, these two realms overlap; there is no fixed line of demarcation between them. People of all spiritual beliefs have the first kind (natural or innate gifts); they may include athletic, musical, artistic, organizational, insightful, or service-oriented talents. Many evaluative tests exist to give handles for grasping your talents. Perhaps the most helpful indicator, however, is to see where success is achieved or fruit is born. When success in school or on the job is realized, that is an indicator that talents are coming to the fore.

Spiritual gifts, on the other hand—that is, those bestowed by the Spirit—are only given to born-again Christians. The Bible says the Holy Spirit "apportions [gifts] to each one individually as he wills" (1 Corinthians 12:11). These gifts include things like teaching, exhorting, prophesying, administration, and healing, and they are for a clear purpose: the edification (building up) of other Christians and for service. Every Christian has one or more gifts as the Spirit determines, and they may vary over time. Spiritual gifts are described in Romans 12, 1 Corinthians 12, and 1 Peter 4, while role gifts (given by Christ to the church) are outlined in Ephesians 4. One way to determine which spiritual gift(s) you have been given is to be involved in service and to look for fruitfulness and the affirmation of others who observe your ministry.

As a caveat, ability and success go hand in hand sometimes, but not always. God may call us to something in our weakness to show us his all-sufficiency. There are plenty of examples of pastors who were called to their roles but who got severely anxious (physically sick) every time they preached, even after years of practice. Moses himself was not a gifted orator (Exodus 4:10), but God still used him—along with his brother as his mouthpiece—to speak to his people.

Both natural and spiritual abilities can be seen, ultimately, as gifts of God that we can use either for his glory as he leads or for our own glory. Ideally, over time, there is a convergence of passion, gladness, success, fruit, and human need in a person's life—but sometimes it takes time to see this convergence, and sometimes it never comes (at least not completely). Our goal should be to discover the talents God has given us as well as we can to be in tune with what we truly enjoy (what makes us tick) and to intentionally seek to merge these in a way that is honoring to the Owner.

Recalibrating

Talents typically emerge—and change—slowly over time. Naturally speaking, we recognize our talents as we mature. Spiritually speaking, we recognize our spiritual gifts after becoming a Christian as we begin to follow God's leading in service to Christ.

It is never too late to take a fresh look at what your talents are, naturally or spiritually.

If you are younger, seek advice and counsel. Find an appropriate mentor who can guide you in the expression of your abilities. If you aspire to missionary work, for instance, talk to your pastor and your family, but also talk to present-day missionaries and read about missionaries of the past—letting all of these voices speak to you, but never to replace the ultimate Counselor, the Holy Spirit.

If you are in midlife, you may have already found the intersection of passion, ability (natural or spiritual), and needs (what pays the bills)—if so, great! If not, we recommend you make use of tool 7. Be open to new leadings and understandings of your gifts.

If you are in the senior season of life, you are in the best position of all, especially if you have been released from commitments to an employer or to a certain (higher) monthly income threshold. Those who are older may find deep human needs just waiting for your talents to meet them. Brainstorm ways you might translate your natural gifts, honed over years of experience, to something you are still physically and mentally able to do and that will honor God. (For example, if you're a retired school teacher or professor, consider teaching Sunday school or starting a discussion/study group in your home.)

Whatever your stage of life, look at yourself as a gifted creation of God. Seek him for his guidance about your calling and for continued understanding about how your talents should be used for his glory.

READ AND REFLECT ON
Colossians 3:17 and Romans 12:6

Prayer: Father, I thank you for the ways you have uniquely wired and gifted me. I ask you to reveal these talents to me and to show me how you want me to use them for your glory and the good of others. Amen.

CHAPTER ELEVEN

STEWARDING TREASURE

Each one must give as he has decided in his heart, not reluctantly or under compulsion, for God loves a cheerful giver.

2 CORINTHIANS 9:7

The 2020 Irish movie *Wild Mountain Thyme* is a romantic comedy-drama set in the lush, green hillsides of the beautiful Emerald Isle. The drama arises when the owner of a small farm decides to will his property to an American nephew instead of his own son, who he believes is not cut out to be a farmer.

The nephew is a high-powered money manager in New York City who knows nothing about running an Irish farm—but who travels to Ireland to visit the property and assess the prospects. Family and friends from adjoining small farms gather for a picnic to meet the nephew, who makes a grand entrance by rolling up in a rented, expensive sports car for the occasion. During the afternoon Adam, the nephew from New York, strikes up a conversation with Rosemary, the attractive, capable young owner of the adjoining farm. Eventually, Adam tells Rosemary she should travel to New York City for a visit.

ROSEMARY   Who would see to my farm [while I'm gone]?

ADAM   You run that [farm] by yourself?

ROSEMARY   Yeah, I do.

ADAM   How many acres do you have?

ROSEMARY   I don't know.

ADAM   How do you not know how many acres of land you have?

ROSEMARY   Because it's just a number.

ADAM   I'm all about numbers. I manage money for a living.

ROSEMARY   Oh, does money need you to manage it?[1]

In the rural, bucolic Irish countryside, where farms have been in families for generations, some official in a deeds office knows how many acres each farm consists of. But in the real world, where boundaries in such settings are marked by streams, ridges, rock walls, hedgerows, and large trees, acreage numbers are often long since forgotten. (At least that's the implication in this movie.)

So we have a balance-to-the-penny Manhattan money manager finding it hard to believe that a rural Irish farmer doesn't know how many acres she owns. We might see these two approaches to money and materials as two ends of a spectrum when it comes to the stewardship of treasure. What kind of attitude should we take toward money: exacting or easy? Rigorous or relaxed? Balanced to the penny or just make sure the bills are paid as needed? Are dollars and acres "just numbers" or does money "need us to manage it"? Perhaps, as is often the case in life, there is value in both perspectives.

TOTAL ACCOUNTABILITY

So far, our discussion of investing our lives wisely has focused on a few fundamental truths:

1. Every human being was created to be a steward of God, and Christians are called to embrace that role.

2. Everything we have comes from and belongs to God. We are simply managers or investors of what he has entrusted to us.

3. With trust comes accountability.

This third truth speaks to a legalistic versus laissez-faire attitude toward money. It's impossible to be accountable for that which we haven't bothered to count or measure. For example, in the well-known parable about the stewardship of money in the Gospels (Matthew 25:14-30), the wealthy man didn't give his servants "some money" with instructions to "do something with it" until he returned. No, he gave one servant five talents (a talent being an ancient Greek monetary measure equivalent to about sixteen years of day-laborer pay), a second servant two talents, and a third servant one talent. Based on the owner's response on his return, he expected that the servants would invest the money (however little or much) and produce a return. In this example, counting and measuring were expected—something that is easy to do with money. In addition, no amount of money was too small to be invested for God's purposes.

We see from this parable that accountability has a test even higher than profit or loss: faithfulness.[2] God has entrusted each of us with some amount of wealth, whether great or small. But he holds us all accountable to himself with how we use our wealth. No matter our financial situation we can use the money we have to honor and worship God by recognizing that he owns all things and that we are stewards of what he has given us.

Consider the three examples of good stewards mentioned in chapter nine: Joseph, Jesus, and Paul. In managing Potiphar's entire household and property, Joseph would have been expected to keep accounts and ledgers to show Potiphar. On the other hand, it is conceivable that Potiphar didn't micromanage the other servants under his charge. Just as God doesn't expect us to record how we spend every second of our day, it is possible to be a good steward without accounting for every single penny. One can be a *good* steward of finances without being a *harsh* steward.

Jesus was 100 percent accountable to God as a servant (Philippians 2:7). Yet Jesus was never anxious or budget-driven. Money wasn't ignored, but it wasn't a driving motivation either. It was a temporal tool. Jesus exemplified what it means to live a faithful but not an anxious life, particularly concerning treasure. His balanced approach to stewardship—being neither too casual nor too uptight about tangible resources—is seen in his interaction with scribes and Pharisees over their one-sided approach to stewardship (Matthew 23:23-24). These Jewish leaders were fastidious about their tithing to God, even counting out their herb seeds to make sure God got his share. While not condemning their painstaking attempts to be good stewards of their culinary treasure, Jesus rebuked them for ignoring "the weightier matters of the law: justice and mercy and faithfulness" (v. 23).

Paul (like Jesus) seems to have had little money of his own. However, he was careful not to be a financial burden on the churches he ministered in (Acts 20:34; 1 Corinthians 4:12; 1 Thessalonians 2:9; 2 Thessalonians 3:8). He plied his trade as a tentmaker when he needed money for his support (Acts 18:3). And he was equally careful when handling other people's money. The funds entrusted to him by the churches in Macedonia and Achaia to meet the needs of the church in Jerusalem he delivered personally, as a steward of their treasures, which he saw safely across land and sea (Romans 15:25-33). The man who identified faithfulness as the chief trait of a good steward worked out that trait in his own life and ministry (1 Corinthians 4:2).

So, is financial stewardship a matter of ledgers or a matter of lifestyle? Both! Faithfulness is the test, and God knows each of our hearts.

LEVERAGING THE TEMPORAL FOR THE ETERNAL

If faithfulness is the test, we better ask the obvious question: faithfulness to what and to whom? Obviously, we're to be faithful to God and to what he expects and values, as best we understand it. But there is a deeper dimension to faithfulness with treasure. Many teachers and preachers note that Jesus talked more about money and possessions than about any other topic. At first, we might conclude this emphasis to be a kind of priority ranking. Money is important; money is tempting; money needs to be handled and managed carefully. That is all true, of course. But it seems that what Jesus is emphasizing is the need to use money toward a deeper end than temporal needs.

As with everything God provides, we have a choice with money: *Do I spend it with a temporal or an eternal mindset?* Money spent on satisfying our ambitions has a short shelf life. Even investments that pay dividends to future generations will ultimately reach their life span when this world ends. But money invested for eternal purposes will never stop paying dividends and is sure to please its ultimate Owner. That's not to say we avoid paying our bills or purchasing necessary material items—God gives us money to meet our needs—but the *way* we do these things matters. We can and should use our finances to give toward what will last: our relationship with God and others.

The teaching of Jesus in Luke 12:13-21 contrasts the use of treasure for temporal or eternal purposes. This parable of the rich fool (which we discussed earlier in relation to sinful presumption about the future) brought a warning from Jesus about greed. Jesus told this parable because a brother wanted his (apparently older) brother to split their inheritance equally, even though in Jewish law the firstborn son received a double portion of the family inheritance (Deuteronomy 21:17). In response Jesus warned him about greed: "One's life does not consist in the abundance of his possessions" (Luke 12:15). Ultimately, the Lord's message was to avoid the error of treasuring the temporal over the eternal.

Jesus immediately illustrated this warning with the parable of the rich fool, centered on a wealthy farmer who had an exceedingly prolific crop. Lacking storage space for his abundance, the farmer decided to tear down his barns and build bigger ones to "store all [his] grain and goods" (Luke 12:18). He then realized that his abundance would allow him to "relax, eat, drink, be merry" for years to come (v. 19). But before his plans were realized, God took his life and called him a fool, asking him, "The things you have prepared, whose will they be?" (v. 20). Jesus concluded the parable with this teaching: "So is the one who lays up treasure for himself and is not rich toward God" (v. 21). That is, such a man is a fool.

Let's be clear: the point of this parable is not that wealthy people die before being able to enjoy their wealth. Neither is the point that it's sinful to accumulate a lot of treasure. The point is that we can either honor or dishonor God in the way we use wealth. Putting our hope in temporal wealth is fleeting, as we have no guarantee concerning the length of our life. To put it colloquially, no one has ever seen a hearse pulling a trailer. *You can't take it with you.*

That is the essence of Jesus' teaching in Matthew 6:19-21. While it's one's life that can be cut short in the parable of the rich fool in Luke 12, it's wealth that can disappear according to Matthew 6. Moths can consume garments, rust can deteriorate metal objects, and thieves can break in and steal money and valuables. Nothing (materially) is guaranteed, except for the fact that God will "supply every need" we have when we have it (Philippians 4:19). Economies, banks, and safeguards are fickle and undependable. We can be rich one day and poor the next.

There is a better plan. "Lay up for yourselves treasures in heaven, where neither moth nor rust destroys and where thieves do not break in and steal. For where your treasure is, there your heart will be also"

(Matthew 6:20-21). Those last words are among the most misapplied in the church. Jesus does not say, "Where your heart is, there your treasure will be." Many preachers have exhorted listeners, "If your heart is right with God, you'll give to God!" While this is true in one sense, that's not the point of this passage in Matthew. Rather, Jesus is pointing out that what we value reveals the state of our heart. If we value money, our treasure is on earth. If we value God, our treasure is in heaven. From this we learn that when we give to God, our heart becomes focused on God. Such is the power of treasure in our life!

Recalibrating our heart requires action: submitting our finances to the will of God and giving generously as he commands. But how exactly do we convert temporal treasures into eternal investments? The fact is it will look different in every person's life. One person may be called to buy a larger house that accommodates a lot of people for hospitality; another may be called to buy a smaller house or to keep renting to free up funds for giving toward missions or other ministries. The point is to hold a loose grip on money and the things it secures for us. Everything should be on the table before God, even funds that may be tied up in a foundation or set aside for kids' inheritance. Why? Because as the saying goes, "If you're giving while you're living, you're knowing where it's going." Or, like those in the investment world like to say, "Money always travels to where it is treated best." And we know God, as the original Owner, will treat our money better than this world will treat it. What we invest with him (for his kingdom purposes) will pay returns that never end, both through the edification of the church and the salvation and building up of individual souls.

PRACTICAL PRINCIPLES FOR SPIRIT-LED GIVING

How does stewarding (God's) treasure look on a practical level?

First, *we shouldn't wait to start saving and investing*. It can be tempting to think when we're younger, "Once I get everything in order—house, mortgage, job, retirement fund—then I will begin giving sacrificially."

But if our temporal wealth is God's, then it's his when we're young as well as when we're older; it's his whether we have little or much. Besides, it's a mistake to think that, once we have *more* money, then it'll be easier to give out of our abundance. Not so! The more we have, the more tempting it can be to hold onto that money and to let ourselves become defined by it (sometimes unconsciously). That's why the only way to desecrate the idol of money is to give it away as an act of worship and trust. Starting this habit of giving is best done early in life (before we've accumulated much to cling to). But regardless of age, today is better than never.

Even when giving becomes a habit, the question of *when* to give remains. There's a delicate balance to strike between the present and the future. The Bible exhorts saving and investing wisely for the future. At the same time, it encourages extravagant and selfless giving, and discourages stinginess and hoarding (see Deuteronomy 15:7-11). We should not store away to the extent that we fail to give what God wants us to give now. A few dollars today might multiply exponentially if invested for future use, but sometimes those few dollars are meant to be invested *today* in some ministry endeavor that will result in eternal impact (such as the salvation of a soul). Only God knows these details.

This brings us to another key point: it's important to *be sensitive to God's leading*. Years ago, seemingly out of the blue, God put two widows on my (Ken's) mind. Independently, he put the same two widows on my wife's mind. Karen and I both felt strongly called to support these women in hopes that the tangible help would enrich the widows' lives and point them to God. We ended up sending annual gifts to those two women over several decades. We gave in the name of Jesus and left the rest in the Lord's hands.

For most people the decision of where to give is closely entwined with the question of tax deductibility. While it is wise to make financial decisions strategically and with due diligence, financial benefits should not be the only factor. Instead, we should seek to give in accordance with the promptings of the Spirit, even if they may seem out of the blue or illogical.

At the same time, not every request is a call from God; not every Christian organization that sends you a solicitation is one you should invest in. In a world where we are bombarded with requests *and* needs, how do we discern where the Spirit is leading us to give? To a large degree the answer is obedience: the more we heed the Spirit's promptings, the more sensitive we will be to his next prompting. If we're unsure about whether to give to a certain place or not, we should pray for specificity in God's guidance.

In addition, any ministry or organization we give to should be—in some way—fulfilling, promoting, and pursuing the Great Commission (Matthew 28:19-20). We can easily do our research and ensure this is the case. We owe it to ourselves and God to know the missions of the organizations we support and how they achieve them. We can look them up via assessment tools like Charity Navigator or make use of philanthropic consultants such as Calvin Edwards and Excellence in Giving. In addition, Ronald Blue Trust offers a robust set of questions for evaluating an organization or project you're considering giving to. These are found in tool 14.

Primarily, we have been discussing the *when* and *where* to give questions, but the *how* is just as important. Following are a few guiding principles.[3]

Give cheerfully and gratefully (2 Corinthians 9:7). Cheerfulness in giving is directly commanded in Scripture, and cheerfulness stems from gratitude for all that God has done for us. When we recognize God's undeserved blessing in our lives, we will naturally come to center our goals on the betterment of others and not merely on ourselves.

Give anonymously (Matthew 6:2-4). Jesus instructs his disciples to give in secret to better ensure we are doing it for the Father's approval and not for public recognition or praise. This manner of giving makes us a conduit of God's grace and helps us avoid giving for manipulative or selfish reasons.

Give consistently (1 Corinthians 16:1-2). Regular disbursements as a discipline help us avoid hoarding resources that can be used for the kingdom. The burden should be on *Why keep this wealth?* instead of on *Why give it away?*

Give harmoniously in marriage, if married (Philippians 2:1-4). Spouses will almost always have different risk thresholds. One may want to give more, the other less. Honor and listen to one another— not only in the area of giving but in all money matters.

Give harmoniously as a church (Philippians 1:5; 4:15). Not only are we to give individually but we're to join with fellow believers in partnership for the gospel (corporate giving). This is a witness to the love and provision of Christ; it is also beneficial on a practical level because of the power of pooled resources.

Give proportionately (2 Corinthians 8:12-14). Give according to ability. Instead of being content with a strict percentage, be willing to increase the proportion given as wealth increases.

Give sacrificially (Luke 21:1-4). If our giving has no bearing on our lifestyle, then we should question whether we're trusting God as the owner of our material wealth. We must be giving up something for it to be truly sacrificial.

RECALIBRATING

Inevitably, everything we accumulate on earth—possessions, property, and so on—is passed on to someone (or to multiple people) when we die. As we age the question of stewarding treasure becomes a stewardship of time issue as well. The more money and *stuff* we have to maintain, the more time it takes to manage. We should be sensitive to God's leading when he may be calling us to simplify or downsize (this can happen even when we're younger!).

Also as we grow older, we increasingly ask what will happen to any leftover treasure after we die. Many people automatically assume that they should leave all they have to their kids. While this *is sometimes* a wise route, it isn't always (cf. Proverbs 17:2, 16). In addition, it is often a good idea for those with wealth tied up in a foundation or similar entity to take a more generous approach to spending their assets while still living— when they can be sure where the money goes—rather than hoping that those after them will maintain the same perspective and priorities.

Judy (see chap. 3) had a difficult time downsizing her possessions but eventually came to know that *Jesus is enough*. The changes she and her husband made inevitably affected her roles—her ability to gather and host family in a central location and her ability to serve friends and other groups with hospitality. She can still serve family and friends, but she's had to accept this senior season in her life as a time for exercising hospitality and love in new and different ways rather than clinging mournfully to her old life.

Stripping away the temporal to focus on the eternal is something God wants to do in all of our lives—not only in the area of material possessions and hospitality and not only when we're older. He is always leading us "further up [and] further in."[4] Pulling ourselves away from our money and material belongings doesn't have to look like a house sale. It may be that God simply wants you to recalibrate *how* you use what you have.

. . . .
READ AND REFLECT ON
Matthew 6:19-24
. . . .

Prayer: Lord, it is so easy to become entangled in the pursuit of treasure in this life. Please keep my heart free from the love of money, and help me always see my tangible resources as yours, not mine. May I use the treasure you've provided for me in a way that is honoring to you—to further your kingdom purposes rather than merely enlarging my little fiefdom. Amen.

TOOL 13: PUTTING YOUR AFFAIRS IN ORDER WITH MEANING AND PURPOSE

My (Ken's) friend Ron Dunn has written an entire book on the subject of "unfinished business."[5] His goal is to help people prepare to leave this life so they don't leave a tangled mess for their loved ones that they have to sort out during the grieving process. This is about planning for the day you're no longer here, to leave order rather than chaos in your wake. (Russ Crosson and his colleagues at Ronald Blue Trust offer similar guidance.)

This type of organization takes great effort and often feels morbid at the time, but it's truly one of the most loving acts you can do for your spouse and other loved ones. And since none of us is guaranteed tomorrow, there's no time better to do this task than now—no matter how young or old you are.

Following are a few of the immensely helpful practical tips Ron offers in his book. (The entire book is worth reading.)

1. Interview your spouse or closest loved one. Ask them the following four questions, and continue to involve them throughout the process of putting your affairs in order.

✦ If I were gone, what would you not know that you wish I had explained?

✦ What type of information would you want to have readily available?

✦ What could I get ready now that would help you get through?

✦ What would you wish I had included in a filing system for easy reference?[6]

2. Establish files. Develop a devoted spot (a physical one—not on your computer), such as a file folder in your filing cabinet, for all important information and documentation that a loved one would need when you're no longer here. (Don't forget to tell them where it is!)

This file should include the following information, which you will want to update regularly, as needed. (This file is also helpful if you become seriously ill and incapacitated.)

✦ *Computer and other passwords.* Usernames, passwords, answers to secret security questions, pin numbers, and any other information needed to unlock everything from your safety deposit box to your computer and other devices to your email accounts and websites where you access your financial institutions, pay your utility bills, access medical and insurance records, and so on.

✦ *Important contacts.* Include contacts for key individuals in your life, from personal-business contacts (e.g., your attorney, accountant, financial/tax adviser, insurance agent(s), real estate adviser) to personal-casual contacts (friends, neighbors, pastor, other family members) to workplace contacts (boss, coworkers). Also include those you wish to be notified about your funeral/memorial service.

✦ *Financial information.*[7] Include a personal financial statement (including cash, retirement, savings, and investments), a list of all key assets and liabilities (loans), and your current budget (estimated), including regular expenses and income. Consider breaking this information into some basic subcategories that make sense for your situation. For example,

- banking and investments
- house/real estate
- car
- insurance
- health
- employment

- charitable giving
- tax filings

✦ *Special information.* Include the location of hidden items and valuables (e.g., jewelry).

✦ *Essential documents (or copies of them and instructions on where to find the originals).* Include birth certificates, social security cards, passports, marriage certificate, adoption papers, citizenship papers, deeds, vehicle titles, last will and testament, living will, trust papers, power of attorney documents, medical directives, military discharges, business agreements, insurance policies, and so on.

✦ *Supplementary homegoing documents.* Include items other than your legal estate-planning documents that will be needed on your death, namely

- funeral/memorial instructions—obituary wording; tombstone engraving; cremation or burial preference; desired burial location (with contact info); songs, music, Scripture, poetry, and so forth to be read or sung; individuals to be part of the service (and their roles), including the officiant, pallbearers, and readers and musicians; organization(s) to receive contributions "in lieu of flowers" (if desired)
- guidance on distribution of possessions that aren't specifically covered in your will—jewelry, collectibles, apparel, books, memorabilia, furnishings, tools, electronics, vehicles, art, and don't forget pets!

3. *Personalize it.* After making your files, the tedious work is done, and you can get creative and personal. Consider adding to your files things like

✦ life letters to family members/friends individually or a collective letter (see tool 17)

✦ a legacy journal or document (see tool 4)

✦ a personal bio

✦ your family history (including a family tree and/or timeline)

✦ personal values

✦ family traditions that you hope are continued by future generations

✦ a list of your favorite Bible verses, books, and songs

4. Legalize it. For the documents mentioned in 2, consult a professional attorney or accountant to make sure all documents get legalized. An unsigned will does not do much good!

TOOL 14: PUTTING YOUR FINANCIAL AFFAIRS IN ORDER

All that we have belongs to God—he is the ultimate owner. To ensure our assets (whether few or many) are used wisely and distributed in a manner that pleases God after we go to be with him, we all need to do a bit of planning. The following four steps are expanded online at recalibrateyourlife.org and designed to help you submit your finances to him.[8]

Four Steps

1. Conduct a current financial assessment.

2. Develop a charitable giving strategy.

3. Make (and officialize) a will and an estate plan.

4. Hold a family conference.

This tool is available at recalibrateyourlife.org.

TOOL 15: A HERITAGE VISION: WHAT ARE YOU LEAVING BEHIND?

This tool, available at recalibrateyourlife.org, provides a template for thinking through your legacy (that is, your vision for your heritage). It encompasses three kinds of capital: financial, spiritual, and social.

CHAPTER TWELVE

STEWARDING TRUTH

Do your best to present yourself to God as one approved, a worker who
has no need to be ashamed, rightly handling the word of truth.

2 TIMOTHY 2:15

When I (Ken) met Antony Flew in Dallas in the 1970s at a worldview conference, I never would've guessed the change that would take place in the man decades later. Once deemed the ablest apologist for atheism in the world (and perhaps in history), Flew was the Richard Dawkins[1] of the 1960s and 1970s. And he remained a staunch advocate of atheism until his early eighties, when he announced a reversal of his position. Contrary to everything he had written and become famous for, he conceded publicly in 2004 that God probably exists after all.

Flew walked in the same circles as C. S. Lewis, and although the two debated from opposite viewpoints, they had something in common: a desire to follow the evidence wherever it leads. (Lewis himself was a convert from atheism, against his own will.) In the early 2000s the evidence, specifically the DNA molecule, led Antony Flew to conclude that an intelligent being (God) must exist. A naturalistic explanation simply couldn't account for such complexity.

Flew went as far as evidence and reason would take him—only surrendering your will, in faith, takes you to Jesus. Still, his openness to the truth was notable. Willing to change a long-held position in the last decade of his life, he was instantly under scrutiny by atheists worldwide. Richard Dawkins even disparaged Flew's reversal in his top-selling *The God Delusion* (2006). Responding to Dawkins in a review of the book, Flew wrote, "This whole business makes all too clear that Dawkins is not interested in the truth as such but is primarily concerned to discredit an ideological opponent by any available means."[2]

Our hope and prayer is that Flew eventually went beyond a deistic belief in God to a belief in the revelatory truth of the Bible. Only God himself knows. Flew's example is still instructive, and it raises a question for us: What do *we* do with the truth we're given? Do we steward it well by being open to its application in our lives? Or do we ignore and neglect it? When God shows us something, such as an area of our character we need to work on, do we respond and apply this truth to our lives right away, or do we tuck it away and think, *I'll deal with that later*?

Stewarding Truth

Time, talent, and treasure are the standard focuses of stewardship that we hear about, and all of us possess them in some amount. But two other areas are equally important, if not more so: truth and relationships. This chapter focuses on truth—God's truth in particular.

We steward time by using time wisely; we steward talent by recognizing and applying our gifts and abilities, and we steward treasure by being accountable for the money and material God has entrusted to us.

> *We steward God's truth by knowing and cherishing*
> *it, and by living and proclaiming it appropriately.*

Truth isn't nearly as tangible or measurable as time, talent, and treasure, but we can identify two key aspects of stewarding God's truth well: (1) recognize truth as a gift from God, and (2) honor and use God's truth in a way that pleases him. In terms of the first there are two obvious manifestations of God's truth that we're to treasure: his living Truth (Jesus) and his written Truth (the Bible).

THE LIVING TRUTH

Pontius Pilate sounded like a postmodern skeptic (think Richard Dawkins, not Antony Flew) when he asked, "What is truth?" (John 18:38). Pilate was speaking to Jesus, but his question seems almost rhetorical as well—perhaps uttered more to himself, even scoffingly. Whatever his tone or intent, Pilate was responding to these words that Jesus had just said to him, "You say that I am a king. For this purpose I was born and for this purpose I have come into the world—to bear witness to the truth. Everyone who is of the truth listens to my voice" (John 18:37). The truth Jesus came into the world to testify to was about God—his identity, purposes, nature, and plans. Jesus himself embodied that truth; he is the living Word of God, whereas the Bible is the written Word of God.

The last part of John 18:37 offers these watershed words: "Everyone who is of the truth listens to my voice." What does it mean to be "of the truth"? *The Message* version says, "Everyone who cares for truth, who has any feeling for the truth, recognizes my voice." The *Amplified Bible* explains, "Everyone who is of the truth [who is a friend of the truth and belongs to the truth] hears *and* listens carefully to My voice." Jesus put it even more directly in John 14:6, where he identifies himself not only as being *on the side of truth*, but *as the truth*: "I am the way, and the truth, and the life. No one comes to the Father except through me."

When we genuinely seek to know God's truth, we will come to know that truth; we will side with both its message and its chief Messenger (the embodiment of God's truth). As a result we will treasure his truth as a gift, as evidenced by our actions—living in light of that truth every day.

To put it succinctly, the first aspect of stewarding God's truth is to nurture our relationship with the One who is truth itself. We won't necessarily understand *all* of God's truth, even in a lifetime, but the closer we walk with Jesus, the more we will know him and the truth he embodies. When we get older, one of the best things for younger Christians to witness is the process of an old saint's ongoing communion and wrestling with God. We're creatures of habit and love our religion, but Christianity is a Person, and we can't get overly comfortable. New growth is always possible.

THE WRITTEN TRUTH

Even before Jesus, the living Word or living Truth, came into this world, God began communicating truth to people in written form. The Old Testament, followed by the New, bore witness to God and his work in the world.

John Robinson was an English Separatist who left England in search of religious freedom in South Holland. He and others like him felt the Church of England had clung to too much of the Roman Catholic traditions. They wanted a purer, less adorned church and became known as Puritans. On July 21, 1620, John Robinson spoke to members of his congregation who were leaving Leiden, South Holland, on the ship *Mayflower* for the New World. They were to go first to pick up more travelers in England and then sail for the land that would become America.

Robinson's plea in his sermon to his flock as they prepared to board the ship concerned their stewardship of God's truth in the New World.

He exhorted them not to follow him or any other human leaders of the European Reformation, but to follow God's Word alone. He said,

> Brethren, we are now quickly to part from one another, and only the God of heaven knows whether I will see your face again. I charge you before God and His blessed angels that you follow me no further than you have seen me follow the Lord Jesus Christ. *I am verily persuaded that the Lord yet has more truth to break forth from His holy Word.*[3]

Robinson—whose words were reminiscent of Paul's "Be imitators of me, as I am of Christ" (1 Corinthians 11:1)—went on to commend "shining lights" like Martin Luther and John Calvin but reminded his listeners that they, as mere humans, "penetrated not into the whole counsel of God."[4] Of course, the same applies to leaders and teachers today. And this discernment between humans' imperfect teaching and God's perfect teaching is a critical aspect of stewarding truth.

As with managing time, talent, and treasure, stewarding truth is a lifelong process of humility, correction, and adjustment. There is tremendous benefit from sitting under the preaching and teaching of those who proclaim God's truth. At the same time, we should never follow any human teacher or preacher as though that person is infallible. Even among the most gifted, well-intentioned witnesses of his truth, there will be error. We human teachers (and authors) are not perfect. As I (Ken) like to advise people, mine the gold and eschew the gravel, and some teachers offer more gravel than others.

Returning to Robinson's words, he not only advised the Puritans to be discerning, following human teachers only insofar as they followed Christ, but he also said he believed God would cause "more truth to break forth from His holy Word." What did he mean? These words capture another aspect of stewardship of truth—and another reason why this area of stewardship is a lifelong process. Hebrews 4:12 says, "The word of God is living and active, sharper than any two-edged sword, piercing to the division of soul and of spirit, of joints and of marrow, and discerning the thoughts and intentions of the heart." God's Word is unchanging, yes. At the same time, his (written) Word is "living and active," meaning it (or rather, its Author—through the power of the Spirit living in us) can speak into our lives, at any moment, to teach, reprove, correct, and instruct us in righteousness (2 Timothy 3:16). This happens individually as well as corporately, when we study God's Word together. We steward this truth that "breaks forth" by humbly accepting its correction in our lives, by always seeking to apply it in all we say and do, and by allowing it to renew our minds so that we are more and more conformed to the image of Christ rather than to the world (Romans 8:29; 12:2).

> *In short, we're to remain lifelong students—*
> *and appliers—of the truth.*

This charge of stewarding truth as a gift of God applies not only to our individual lives but to our corporate lives. Churches (and we as its members) have to be vigilant to guard God's truth and resist the culture's attempts to encroach on the boundaries set up in his Word. This requires faithful studying, teaching, and preaching, week after week.

SPEAKING AND LIVING THE TRUTH

In our pursuit and application of truth in our lives, we tend to move through the following three stages.

Childhood/youth. Childhood is the season for discovering God's truth for the first time. During this season we study, study, study—often taking in the Scriptures with a voracious appetite. Yes, we can and should share his truth during this season, but we should always do so humbly, knowing we still have much to learn ourselves. Just as human children need the correction and mentoring of a parent, young believers need mature teachers and mentors to help them grow in their knowledge and understanding of the truth.

Middle age. Middle age is the season for applying truth personally, especially to areas (such as family life and work) where we may have failed to apply it fully thus far. We continue to read and study during this period, going deeper than we did initially and depending more and more on the Spirit and less on human teachers. We may become a mentor to a few others even as we still need mentoring ourselves.

Old age. Old age is the season for being a beacon of truth to rising generations and to living a life built on a foundation of unchanging truth as revealed in Christ (the living Word) and in God's written Word. At this stage believers will still have peers in the faith and, if possible, older believers mentoring them (even if they're deceased authors), but they have become better equipped to pass along truth to those younger in the faith and should seize the opportunities to do so. Of course, humility is still needed, especially given Paul's warning that knowledge "puffs up" (1 Corinthians 8:1), as is time in God's Word (whose depths can never be fully plumbed as long as we live).

These three stages are seasons of varying lengths, and they are sometimes but not always correlated with chronological age. Ideally, we are exposed to the truth when we are young and accept it early in life. But this doesn't always happen, and it is by God's design that every person is on his or her timetable. Some believers reach a high level of maturity early in life, while others are still in their youth, spiritually speaking, when they are chronologically older.

Regardless of age—spiritually and chronologically—the accumulation of truth and the responsible stewardship of it is one of the most valuable and desirable things we can do, affecting all areas of life (Psalm 19:9-11).

But how exactly do we steward truth? As we possess more of it, how do we pass it on—investing it in others? Here are a few ways:

1. Preach/proclaim the truth (2 Timothy 4:2).

2. Practice the truth that you teach or preach so that you do not discredit yourself (Titus 2:7).

3. Witness to the truth with boldness and without shame (Luke 9:26; Romans 1:16; 10:14-15; Philippians 1:20-21; 2 Timothy 1:8).

4. Teach the truth to edify fellow believers (1 Corinthians 12:28; Ephesians 4:11; Colossians 1:28; 3:16; 1 Timothy 4:13).

5. Handle the truth correctly (1 Timothy 4:16; 2 Timothy 2:15).

6. Watch for false teaching and false teachers, who distort or otherwise fail to accurately proclaim the truth (1 Timothy 6:3; Hebrews 13:9; 2 Peter 2:1; 2 John 1:10).

7. Train more teachers of the truth (2 Timothy 2:2).

8. Teach in accordance with Scripture, not to please people or their passions (2 Timothy 4:3; Titus 2:1).

9. Communicate the truth to others with gentleness and respect; do not be quarrelsome when proclaiming it (2 Timothy 2:25; 1 Peter 3:15).

There are many more points we could add. It's important to remember that it's not only the content of the truth that is important but also how—the manner and timing—we communicate it. Sometimes we should restrain from speaking truth, never out of timidity or fear but out of discernment as we attune ourselves to the promptings of God. When evangelizing it's particularly important to avoid hard-sell methods and scare tactics. If we don't avoid these, they can put up barriers that cause nonbelievers to reject the real thing.[5]

The Bible is clear that we are to be faithful witnesses to the truth, unafraid to share it and determined to live it out by the power of God's Spirit. It is also clear that even when we are faithful some people will simply not accept the truth, or they may initially accept it but later fall away from or doubt it (as illustrated by the various types of soil and responses to God's Word in the parable of the sower [Matthew 13:1-9, 18-23]). It is not our responsibility to make his truth stick, that is, to make someone believe and embrace it; that is God's territory. We can be good stewards of his truth even when others reject our message— in fact, they often will.

RECALIBRATING

The great casualty of our postmodern era is the belief in the existence of truth. Even as followers of Christ we may be unconsciously infected with this mindset, leading us to minimize or even abandon the truths of the Bible. What we think and believe may start to be replaced by what we feel, experience, and desire. It is difficult to live in a culture of "*my* truth" without that culture having an impact on one's sense of *the* truth.

Recalibration can help us separate truth from feelings and see where we might have come to accept the lies of our culture (perhaps without even realizing it). Recalibrating in this area may entail a larger investigation into the truth claims of Christianity (such as the case for the resurrection or some other area of apologetics). Most basically, it's good to review the truths *of first importance* we hold to: "Christ died for our sins in accordance with the Scriptures, . . . was buried, . . . [and] was raised on the third day in accordance with the Scriptures" (1 Corinthians 15:3-4). In this passage Paul goes on to list Christ's myriad appearances after his resurrection. All of these truths, Paul says, he received and was now passing down to the Corinthians (and us); we in turn are to pass them down to the next generation of believers (v. 3).

Our friend Mary Virginia is a wonderful model of this sagacious stewarding of truth. Inspired in part by our interview questions for this book, she decided to compile a book for her children. This book gives aspects of her life and personal testimony along with highlights of the gospel story. The dedication reads, in part,

I am so blessed to have forebears who loved the Lord Jesus and his word and saw that it was passed to the next generation. I am also blessed to have sat at the feet of many godly teachers through the years who God used to shape my belief system that I taught as I learned. At age eighty-eight I am still learning.

So it is with a grateful heart that I dedicate these lessons to my five beautiful grandchildren . . . lessons that I have learned, taught, and tried to live by. . . .

I pass them on to you with prayers that you will know your Creator and know the joy of walking with him as you make your journey through life.

In an age of digital everything, imagine the impact such a personalized print book is likely to have on these five grandchildren—and those who come after them! And anyone can do a similar thing for their loved ones (tool 4 and tool 1 are specifically designed to help you do so).

Any society, family, church, or leader is just one generation away from chaos if it chooses not to pursue or pass on God's truth (Judges 2:6-13). Let us take care to build bridges to members of the next generation by investing God's truth in them at any opportunity we get.

READ AND REFLECT ON
John 8:31

Prayer: Father, I thank you for the gift of your Word—both the Bible and the Word made flesh in Jesus Christ. May I seek your truth eagerly, follow it devotedly, live it out consistently, proclaim it boldly, and thus steward it faithfully. Amen.

CHAPTER THIRTEEN

STEWARDING
RELATIONSHIPS

As we have opportunity, let us do good to everyone, and
especially to those who are of the household of faith.

GALATIANS 6:10

In heaven there will be untold numbers who were won to Christ in the past three centuries through the preaching of Dwight L. Moody, Billy Sunday, and Billy Graham. These billions of people will seek out a man named Edward Kimball to thank him.

If you've never heard of Kimball, you're not alone. But his legacy proves what a "nobody" on earth can do when he cares about people and God's kingdom.

The young Sunday school teacher befriended a teenager in Chicago in 1855; he visited him at the shoe store where the teen worked, and shared the gospel with him. Kimball nurtured the young man's faith in the Sunday school class he taught. That young man was Moody, who went on to spend his life preaching the gospel on both sides of the Atlantic, winning thousands to Christ for eternity.

From there Kimball's influence continued to domino:

1. Moody shared Christ with a man named F. B. Meyer.
2. F. B. Meyer's preaching led to the conversion of J. Wilbur Chapman.
3. Chapman's preaching led to the conversion of Billy Sunday.
4. Mordecai Ham was converted at a Billy Sunday meeting.
5. Billy Graham was converted at a Ham meeting.
6. Graham preached the gospel face-to-face to more people than anyone else in history.

What if Kimball hadn't signed up to teach Sunday school? How many people would not have heard the life-saving message of Jesus? Kimball was a good steward of a seemingly small relationship that bore eternal fruit forever. Ready and willing to invest in the relationships in front of him, no matter how small or large the investment seemed at the time, he trusted God with the results of his work.

We have said that investing our time, talent, and treasure are all temporal stewardship goals. They are worthy and important, but eternal only insofar as they are leveraged for the sake of things that last beyond this lifetime. The stewardship of truth and relationships, by contrast, have a straight line drawn from this life into eternity. This is because God's Word and people are the only two things on this earth that are truly eternal.

In chapter four we discussed the priority of people and relationships in life. Because people are of infinite worth in God's sight, they should be in ours as well. To understand better how to steward relationships, a visual can be helpful.

THE THREE CIRCLES OF RELATIONSHIPS

Most of us place the highest importance on our nuclear or biological family—and rightly so, for if we do not properly care for those in our household (spouse, children), then our witness is tarnished by hypocrisy. But the Bible gives us reason to expand our stewardship focus. Doing so can be at the center of recalibrating.

In particular, Paul suggests two additional relationship circles in Galatians 6:10: "So then, as we have opportunity, let us do good to everyone, and especially to those who are of the household of faith." If we add these two circles to the family circle, we have three concentric circles of stewardship responsibility: the family circle (the smallest), the faith circle, and the human circle (see fig. 14.1).

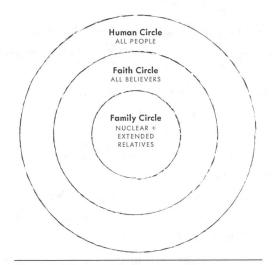

Figure 14.1. Three circles of relationships

The human circle. Working from the outside in, let's consider the human circle first. In Acts 17 Paul speaks with Epicurean and Stoic philosophers of the Areopagus (council) in Athens. These philosophers met regularly to discuss the latest religious and philo-sophical ideas (vv. 18-21). Paul was motivated by his distress at seeing a city filled with idols (v. 16). So, what he said to them would have flown in the face of their pantheon-of-gods mindset: "The God who made the world and everything in it . . . made from one man every nation of mankind to live on all the face of the earth"

(vv. 24, 26). In this passage, Paul is referencing the Genesis creation account along with other parts of Scripture, such as Deuteronomy 32:8 and 1 Chronicles 1:1, where Adam is identified as the head of the human race. Without going into all the other implications of Paul's words, for now we can use them to apply the word *family* to the human race—an extended network of relatives descended from a common ancestor.

This human family is huge (just the number alive today is now approaching eight billion); thus, each of us only has relationships with a minuscule minority of this outer circle. Yet we are still linked as image-bearers made by God and descended from Adam.

Consider how you might react when meeting a long-lost relative for the first time. Despite not knowing each other, there would be an immediate sense of connection, a bond that would likely grow as you trace through the family tree and history together. What if we were to consider every stranger (new person) we meet with a similar attitude? Paul in Galatians, remember, says we are to "do good to everyone"— that is, anyone in the human family—when we have the opportunity. This strikes at the heart of our stewardship responsibility: we are to treat anyone we encounter in exactly the way God (the Creator-Owner) would treat them. We imitate Christ and his love by humbly considering others' interests and by maintaining an attitude of "affection and sympathy" toward them (Philippians 2:1-4). This applies to encounters with people we know well (friends, neighbors, co-workers, and the like) as well as with those we encounter only briefly—a seatmate on an airplane, a mechanic at the car garage, the clerk who rings up our purchase in a store. If we believe that all appointments in life are divine appointments, then we have a responsibility to view every one of these relationships as important ("Lord, is there something I can do at this moment, however long, to represent you well before this person—to consider his or her interests above my own?").

The faith circle. The second layer of relational stewardship is the circle of faith or what Paul calls "the household of the faith." Local congregations or churches are, of course, the *visible* manifestation of this circle, which includes the *invisible* body of all believers that transcends geography and time.

When writing letters to first-century Christians and churches, the apostles focused on two things: doctrine and relationships. Yes, there was theology to teach and clarify, especially to Gentiles with no Old Testament backgrounds. But relationships—the heart of real life on the ground—were just as challenging. We may think identity politics is a twenty-first-century idea, but it is not. That's why Paul had to write words such as Galatians 3:28: "There is neither Jew nor Greek, there is neither slave nor free, there is no male and female, for you are all one in Christ Jesus."[1] The idea of viewing—and therefore treating—all Christians the same was challenging.

Paul's well-known metaphor of the body of Christ illustrates *why* we are to take care of one another: "We, though many, are one body in Christ, and individually members one of another" (Romans 12:5). Paul says individual Christians are like the various organs and limbs in the body. When one is weak, the whole is weaker; when one is strong, the whole is stronger. Being good stewards of our relationships in the circle of faith leads to a healthier and stronger body, in terms of both the individual parts and the whole. One way we steward well relationships with other believers is by being channels of God's love and stewards or administrators of God's grace (1 Peter 4:10; Ephesians 3:2).

To subdivide Paul's metaphor of the body to a finer level, think of individual human beings as cells in the body of humanity, and individual Christians as cells in the body of Christ. Just as cells work together to promote health, so we can do the same for humanity and for Christ's body, the church. Dozens of times the phrase *one another* appears in the New Testament Epistles. All of these offer specific examples of how we are commanded to steward or manage our relationships with other believers. These commands were originally given in the context of local churches, to help groups of believers (like the believers at Corinth or Ephesus) know how to behave toward one another.

The family circle. The third group of relationships we're to steward is the family circle. This includes biologically related members of our nuclear and extended families as well as those who have been adopted and grafted in other ways. Most of us need fewer instructions and reminders about our responsibilities in this circle than with the other two. Innately, we know that the care of our family relationships should be a high priority. Paul wrote to Timothy, "If anyone does not provide for his own, and especially for those of his household, he has denied the faith and is worse than an unbeliever" (1 Timothy 5:8 NASB).

Two key terms in the biblical theology of relationships are the Hebrew *hesed* (loyal love) and Greek *agapē* (unconditional or loyal love). The notion of loyal love is a Judeo-Christian one, not a pagan one. In a day when spouses and children could be abandoned on a whim with no recourse, Paul wrote that not being loyally loving to one's family makes him or her worse than a pagan. Why worse? Because we know better! From Genesis to Revelation we have the loyal love of God demonstrated to us. And stewards are always attuned to what the owner desires—to what he would do. If the owner manifests loyal love, then so should the steward. Not to do so is to deny the faith we profess.

TOOL 16: THE ONE ANOTHERS: HOW TO INVEST IN RELATIONSHIPS

This tool is available at recalibrateyourlife.org.

CHRISTLIKE COMPASSION

Cain, son of Adam and Eve, stained the human record early on by failing to be a good steward of his relationships. Out of jealousy, envy, or some other ill-founded feeling, Cain murdered his brother Abel (Genesis 4:8). When God confronted Cain about his brother's absence, Cain lied, saying, "I do not know [where Abel is]; am I my brother's keeper?" (v. 9). Based on God's judgment of Cain (vv. 11-12), the answer to Cain's question was a resounding yes. Cain *was* called to steward his relationship with Abel well—but he didn't; he failed to care for his brother the way God cared for him, and he was punished for it.

God's response to Cain provides a guide for the relationships in our own lives. We are a steward of our relationships within the three circles of figure 14.1: the human family, the Christian family, and our bloodline family. Wherever God has placed us vis-à-vis all three of these circles, we have stewardship responsibilities.

In chapter four we spoke of the need to prioritize people and to live without regrets in our relationships. Paul's words in Ephesians 4:32 speak to the overarching approach we're to have in proactively stewarding relationships—an approach that contrasts starkly with that of the hard-hearted, envious Cain: "Be kind to one another, tenderhearted, forgiving one other, as God in Christ forgave you." In other words take the same attitude toward other people that God has taken toward you. Through Christ, God has shown undeserved forgiveness, kindness, and compassion toward us. And our task is to show the same to others.

Patrick, an American missionary in Paris, tells of a French man, Henri, he met and invited (along with a few others) to come to his place every Sunday night to watch American football. Henri never missed a gathering over two years, and he began to come around other times too—dropping by Patrick's apartment, texting, and calling throughout the week. A friend noted the pattern and remarked to

Patrick, "Doesn't Henri annoy you? He's *always* around!" Patrick responded, "Well, here's the thing: Henri is treasured by God, and so I believe he should be treasured by me too."

Patrick and his family are stationed in Paris because of their heart for the lost. Despite being known as the City of Lights, Paris is a post-Christian, spiritually dark place with low access to the gospel, he explains. From Scripture, especially Luke 15, we know "lost people matter to God, and he wants them to be found," as Patrick puts it—summarizing the heart behind their ministry. This idea is what drives him to show warm hospitality to and develop relationships with people like Henri; his goal is to eventually share the gospel not only with actions but with words. Henri, he said, once told him, "Patrick, you have a lot of people in your life, but for me, *you're it*. I don't have anyone else." No wonder this incredibly lonely man shed tears after Patrick and his family baked him a cake on his birthday. "I can't remember the last time anyone sang happy birthday to me," Henri said.[2]

How many of us treat every lost person we encounter, every relationship with a nonbeliever, in a similar manner—*treasuring them* because God treasures them, as Patrick does with Henri? Make no mistake, such an approach will revolutionize your relationships—and your life. Most of us default to giving people what we think they deserve, to what they have given us. Instead, while we still have the opportunity, we're called to give them better than they deserve because God has given us better than we deserve.

A judgment day is coming, however (Hebrews 9:27); the graves will empty, and each person will go either to eternal life or to eternal separation from God (John 5:28-29). At that point we will no longer have the opportunity to demonstrate and proclaim the gospel. Thus, while we still have the time we must imitate Christ in how we treat others—including our brothers and sisters in the faith as well as those who don't know him.

RECALIBRATING

Although times have changed with digital technology, most of us cross paths with numerous people every day (some through written or digital means, of course). As we age, we may leave home less often, have less energy to expend on relationships, or even be bound to a single room or bed. But whether our social circles are large and growing or small and shrinking, the question is the same: *How can I make a lasting investment in others' lives?*

I (Ken) spoke at two assisted-living facilities in Atlanta a few years ago. Tenants of these places sometimes wonder, usually silently to themselves, *Why am I still here?* As I spoke to the groups, I emphasized that none of them are in a waiting room, as they might suppose, waiting to graduate to the next life. Rather, as long as they have life and breath, they have a purpose, and God can use them. As I explained, we can all have a lifelong ministry to others because *every person can do three things for others*:

1. love them

2. serve them

3. pray for them

This trio echoes the call of Galatians 6:10: "As we have opportunity, let us do good to everyone, and especially to those who are of the household of the faith." As I walked out of my talks to those two groups, I could tell several in the audience got it. They left the chapel with a little extra pep in their step.

These three things can be done anywhere, anytime, regardless of the state of our health, assuming we have no serious, organic problem that affects our cognition.

One lady does all three of these things at once in what she calls her "desk ministry." This ministry occupies hours of her week—sometimes hours each day. She spends quiet moments, hidden from most people, simply writing notes to encourage, counsel, and comfort others in an age where the art of letter writing has all but vanished. What a tremendous way to serve God in the capacity she is able!

Remember, Jesus frequently stopped his entire day to tend to a single person's need—whether healing an affliction or answering a question—even if that person was considered an outcast or less important to others in his society. This is what Edward Kimball did as well. A salesman, he taught Sunday school on the side. Yet his faithful stewardship had epic ramifications.

We are called to the same mindset, viewing all of our relationships and encounters with people as orchestrated in some way by God.

READ AND REFLECT ON
2 Timothy 4:1-8

Prayer: Heavenly Father, thank you for loving me when I didn't deserve it, for giving me better than I deserve in Christ. Help me share your love with everyone I meet, starting with those I live with and see every day and ending with those with whom I may have only a brief exchange. Use me to help others come to know you, and remind me that no relationship or encounter is too insignificant to make a tremendous difference for your kingdom. Amen.

TOOL 17: WRITING LIFE LETTERS

My (Ken's) friend Ron Dunn advises, "Take the appropriate time to personalize individual letters sharing thoughts and advice with each of those closest to you. These lasting thoughts and words of advice should come from your heart, your experience and your best desires."[3]

A letter may be

✦ individualized and directed to a single loved one

✦ an overall message to all family members (or a group of them, such as all of your children)

✦ a combination of an individualized and group message

Following are some ideas for what to include.[4] *A note on format:* handwritten letters are always more personal and touching. At the same time, keep in mind that you may want to amend these letters over time, and thus it may be better to put them in a digital format that you can easily edit. Just make sure to back up the electronic file(s) in a safe place and *also print a physical copy* of the current version of the letter(s) and keep them in your important homegoing files (e.g., wherever you keep your estate plan/will).

Overall message. This message is to your whole surviving family or a group of family members/loved ones. It might include

✦ your conversion story/testimony (include both how you came to faith and details on your journey with Christ after conversion)

✦ your life verse(s)

✦ life lessons

✦ encouragement regarding life focus and purpose

✦ final words of appreciation and perspective

✦ summary of your hope

Individualized message. Instead of or in addition to the overall message, this is aimed at a single person and might include

✦ characteristics and strengths you observe in that person

✦ encouragement to exercise their gifts and use them to God's glory

✦ favorite memories you have involving that person

✦ verses from God's Word specifically selected for that person

✦ your prayer for that person

✦ your blessing on that person

LIVING SO THAT THE BEST IS YET TO COME

Has this world been so kind to you that you should leave with regret? There are better things ahead than any we leave behind.

C. S. LEWIS, *LETTERS TO AN AMERICAN LADY*

While working on this book we stumbled on a short video about butterflies, using the wonder of twenty-first-century technology to reveal details of these magnificent creatures that are invisible to the unaided human eye. The video's microscopic perspective moves from feature to feature of a butterfly's body, which is "packed with microscopic systems and biological machines that keep it alive, airborne, and stunningly beautiful."[1] In the video the narrator notes how easy it can be to marvel at the grandiose beauty in God's creation—the sweeping majesty of a mountain range or the grandeur of an enormous waterfall. We can easily forget, ignore, or become indifferent to the "subtle miracles [that] unfold each day with little or no recognition from the outside world."[2] For instance, we might see a butterfly in our front yard, flitting from plant to plant, and take its effortless flight for granted. Most of us are ignorant of the amazing process that enables each flap of its wings.

Likewise, it can be easy (and tempting) to marvel at the lives of well-known Christians—pastors, missionaries, community leaders, social changemakers past and present—and stand amazed by the legacy they have built or are building. We may then wonder about, even downplay, our role in God's bigger story. We *want* our lives to count, to matter in a lasting way, but we worry they won't, that we'll soon be forgotten.

Yet what if every single follower of Jesus bears a largely hidden-to-the-world, yet stunningly miraculous, beauty and purpose—intricately fine-tuned to the (spiritually) microscopic level, with the design of making an eternal difference in the kingdom of God? What if we simply lived and repeatedly recalibrated as he designed us—manifesting the glory of our Creator, fulfilling the unique purpose he made us for and stewarding every resource he has given in accordance with that purpose rather than fixating on whether *we* will be noticed or honored down through human history? It's doubtful Edward Kimball imagined his small ministry having an impact on billions of souls; he was just an ordinary man, faithful to God's calling, committed to investing in a few people, and ready to seize the *kairos* opportunities in front of him.

IRREMOVABLE PAGES OF GOD'S BOOK

In the 1987 film *84 Charing Cross Road* one of the main characters, played by Anne Bancroft, reads a lesser-known excerpt of John Donne's "Meditation 17." The words are apropos to the idea of legacy:

> All mankind is of one author, and is one volume; when one man
> dies, one chapter is not torn out of the book, but translated into
> a better language; and every chapter must be so translated; God
> employs several translators; some pieces are translated by age,
> some by sickness, some by war, some by justice; but God's hand

is in every translation; and his hand shall bind up all our scattered leaves again, for that library where every book shall lie open to one another.[3]

These words paint a beautiful picture of the interconnectedness of each generation. All of us are necessary parts (pages) in the book God is writing of the history of humanity. Not one of us will fall out or be torn out. Of course, this is not to advocate universalism—the Bible is clear: some people will go on to live with God forever while others will be condemned eternally. But among those who have trusted Christ, every single one of us is an indispensable part of the body, the church, that God has created. Every "living stone" of this metaphorical building (of which Christ is the chief cornerstone) is vital and part of a living legacy that will last forever (1 Peter 2:5-7). When we take God at his word, we will heed his call to persevere to the end in fulfilling whatever part he has given us. We will recalibrate often to ensure we are staying on course, honoring him every season of our lives.

Every single believer has a unique role in making God's name known from one generation to the next. We are all generational links. Yet, to live, transition, and finish well in life, we must treasure what God treasures— valuing and pursuing the eternal over the temporal. And for this to happen and to *continue* to happen in your life, regular recalibration is necessary. It's simply too easy for the gravity of this world to entice any of us back without frequently reexamining what we are treasuring.

One of the intergenerational translators Donne's meditation mentions is sickness. Another is age, another war. The very things that we would consider to be the most undesirable, difficult aspects of life are those God often uses to translate his message from our lives to others'. Suffering, like death, is one of the great uniters in life—enabling us to relate to one another, regardless of age or stage; difficulties also pave a way for us to communicate the priority of the eternal over the temporal.

I (Jenny) recall distinctly a time several years ago when my parents sat my two siblings and me down for a family gathering, and they spent an evening simply relating the faithfulness of God to our family in the past. After handing us each a copy of Psalm 91, they recounted major moments of struggle, particularly in the financial and employment areas of life, and then explained how God provided for us every single time. Although much of what they related I was already aware of because I am the firstborn (by a long shot), I was struck by the simultaneous intentionality and naturalness of the meeting. *I will do this one day too,* I thought. The gathering required no formal or legal efforts, no fancy planning—just a couple willing to "lie open to one another" and their children (as Donne puts it), pointing us to the One we owe all things to.

AN APPETITE FOR HEAVEN

When we are younger and a loved one passes away (whether it's a grandparent or parent or someone else), it is a very common and very human reaction to want those people back with us again. Many Christians celebrate the graduation of a fellow brother or sister in the faith to heaven while grieving the loss of that person's presence on earth. It's as if a part of *us* dies when someone close to us dies—leaving an irreplaceable gap, a hole, in our lives.

As we get older a shift happens. Instead of looking ahead to a future on earth without some of the people we have known and loved most, we begin to look *back* more and wish we could stay with our kids or those we love who are younger than us. We grieve the loss of friends, and sometimes we can become so consumed with this sorrow that it paralyzes us from living fully in the present. We dwell on, even live in, our memories, and as a consequence we can become ineffective as *current* witnesses and agents of God's love and truth.

Being older myself and having had many relatives and friends pass on to the next life, I (Ken) understand the emotional challenges of aging. And not all reflection on the past is bad. At the same time I have become increasingly convinced that the problem most of us have as we age is that we are—as C. S. Lewis put it in this chapter's epigraph—living *too much* in the past, marinating in regret, and we are not fully convinced in our hearts and minds that what lies ahead truly is better (infinitely better) than what lies behind. Thus, we do not long for our true, eternal home as we should. If we did, would we not spend much more time and energy hoping, praying, and acting in such a way that the next generation will join *us* after we die? Instead, we spend more time than we should wishing we could relive our lives or stay behind with those we love.

One of the most important ways I am recalibrating regularly is by consciously cultivating my appetite for the eternal. My wife, Karen, and I do this together. We take nature walks and admire creation, allowing the beauty and order to draw us upward and spark our longings for the One who promises an even better final home. We also do little thought experiments together, discussing what we think heaven will be like, who we'll see there, what we will talk about, what we will create together, and so on. We imagine the perfect community of heaven, where we will enjoy new capacities, new relationships, new pleasures, new songs, *new everything*—all of which will make our old capacities, old relationships, and old treasures pale in comparison.

I like to use the lists in figure 15.1 as a reminder of the features of our final home.

Won't have	**Will have**
✦ the world	✦ resurrected world
✦ the flesh	✦ resurrected bodies
✦ the devil/demons	✦ unbounded future as
✦ death, sickness,	gardeners of the new
mourning, aging,	creation
pain	✦ enhanced relational
	capacity
	✦ expanding vision of God

Figure 15.1. Cultivating an appetite for heaven

The Old Testament character Job seemed to grasp how puny our human imaginations of our future in heaven are: "Behold, these are but the outskirts of his ways," Job declared, "and how small a whisper do we hear of him!" (Job 26:14). Indeed, we glimpse only the edges of God's ways here on earth, but even a faint hint of his glory and goodness should cause our regrets to fade and our longings to grow—*even when our time is running out and our bodies are wearing out.*

Most of us sit before a gigantic feast God has prepared for us and fail to eat (or to take more than a nibble). When we take time to cultivate an appetite for the eternal, we will find that not only do temporal things fade in their significance to us, but the transitions and challenges of life will be less likely to destabilize us or even throw us overboard. Why? Because our hope is transferred and our heavenly citizenship is secure; we are happy pilgrims en route to a better country. We are genuinely looking forward to what is to come.

LIVING SO THE BEST IS YET TO COME

Despite age and outward appearances, followers of Jesus can say we're winding *up*, not *down*, in life—we're on an incline toward a *better* quality of life, not in decline (as so many of us tend to view aging). Our earthly suits may be wearing out, but, as Paul put it, "our inner self is being renewed day by day" (2 Corinthians 4:16).

Jonathan Edwards, in his first sermon ever preached, spoke of the realities of suffering, the truth that God has our best end in mind, and the fact that the best is yet to come.[4] In an early version of this book our working subtitle was "Navigating the Stages of Life so That the Best Is Yet to Come," based on the third point in Edwards's sermon. In one sense the best is always yet to come for believers because eternal life with God is our future. Nothing—not even the best moments of our lives on earth—will compare to the joy we have when we meet God face-to-face and spend eternity communing with him and his people.

However, is the best always yet to come on earth? Some resonate with this idea while others don't. One eighty-seven-year-old lady seems to understand what Edwards was getting at:

> Physical ailments, diminishing eyesight and hearing, the aging brain all take away from this being "the best" time of life. What is the best is I know [God] better, I see him at every turn, and each day I am closer to *the Best*, which is "when I see him, I shall be like him, for I shall see him as he is" (1 John 3:2). In my opinion, one season of life is not better than the other. Each one is different and has its "best" part. And each is a part of God growing us into his likeness. That being said, of course, the closer we grow to him, the better life gets.

What a contrast this lady's vision is from the one cast by Mitch in *City Slickers*! Yes, life on earth is hard, but genuine life in Christ is *always* good and is always getting better. How many of us see our lives this way—with the potential of getting better and better even after we're "over the hill," when our bodies are aching and breaking and we're perhaps more alone than ever in this earthly pilgrimage? Yet, if we have such a growing love and hunger for the Lord that our relationship with *him* becomes the measure of our quality of life, then no physical or external factors can diminish the inner peace and joy he gives.

CHRIST THE VICTOR

In her final months on earth Corrie ten Boom was virtually helpless, needing assistance just to turn over in her bed. She could barely speak, and since her last stroke two-plus years before, she had become skin and bone. But her caregiver Pam Rosewell "marveled . . . at the communication that is possible in silence." She relates some of those final moments with Tante Corrie:

> Suddenly, she [Corrie] surprised me by saying a word in Dutch [ten Boom's native language]: *"Blij"* ("Happy," more literally, "joyful").

"Are you happy, Tante Corrie?"

"*Ja* [yes]."

She made a certain movement with her mouth, which I had come to recognize as a desire to sing. I began to sing one of her favorite Dutch hymns and she joined in very slowly, but as quickly as her old heart would allow.[5]

The hymn they sang together in Dutch was translated thus:

Praise God with waves of joy.

You, my soul, have such cause to be thankful.

For as long as I live I will dedicate my psalms to His praise,

As long as I see light I will extol God in my song.[6]

Rosewell describes how, on the morning of ten Boom's ninety-first birthday, April 15, 1983, Tante Corrie breathed her last. "There were no heavenly revelations. The room was quiet and peaceful just before she left us. It was quiet and peaceful after she left us."[7] Today, her grave is marked with her name, her birth and death dates, and three simple words: "Jesus Is Victor."

Indeed, Christ is victor. He has overcome. There is nothing to fear— in life or death. As long as we draw breath, our lives can declare that message. And when we die, that message lingers on, in heaven and on earth, as we're ushered into the everlasting joy and presence of our loving Father.

KEEPING ON THE PATH

As we prepare for that day when we see him face-to-face, we may be confident of our final destination while uncertain of the next steps on the journey. Ours is a journey full of twists and turns, never a straight path. The recalibration process encourages us to ask three questions:

Where have I been?

Where am I now?

Where do I go from here?

Asking these questions during times of transition or crisis and taking them to the Lord and his Word will help us navigate these moments (whether they're grief-filled, joyful, or something in between) with hope and purpose. We also benefit from asking these questions as a part of the regular rhythm of our life, as such questions often spur the recollection and renewal necessary to prompt spiritual growth and even redirection.

In my (Ken's) current phase of life, many of my mentors are long since dead, and I spend significant time mentoring others of various ages. I've taken at least a dozen through the recalibration process in recent years. This is a privilege and joy for me; I desire to give away what I've been given. I want to be a transgenerational sage who conveys and communicates godly wisdom to people who are open to ongoing growth and development. I enjoy helping people to see patterns in their lives, connect the dots, and view their lives with fresh eyes.

As a grateful recipient of this wisdom (from Ken as well as other sages in my life), I (Jenny) have been challenged to not simply keep pushing forward, nose to the grindstone, without asking the questions of purpose, legacy, and stewardship that seem to hit many of us around midlife. *If my life is almost half over, am I using my time and talent wisely on things that make an eternal impact? Am I guilty of idealizing retirement from a worldly perspective?*

In this journey of life we need each other—to spur us on, to remind us how our paths meet his "larger way" (as Bilbo sang in *The Lord of the Rings*), a way that ends in unspeakable glory and pleasure forevermore. The question is, Are we ready for that final transition?

. . . .
READ AND REFLECT ON
Revelation 21:1-7
. . . .

Prayer: Lord, I cannot fathom all that you have planned for me and your people as a whole. I only know that our future with you is better than I can imagine; indeed, dwelling with you is the best place we can be.

Please cultivate in me an appetite for the eternal. Replace my hunger for the things of this world with hunger for you and your Word. Make me a link between generations, so that more and more will stand in your presence one day to proclaim your excellencies and goodness. Amen.

TOOL 18: WRITING YOUR OWN EULOGY

The exercise of writing your eulogy can feel awkward and morbid to some; to others it feels self-promoting or pompous. But drafting your eulogy (a tribute to honor or celebrate a person's life) can also be one practical way to illuminate—for yourself if for nobody else—what you'd like to be remembered and known for; in other words, what are you living for—what are *you* all about in terms of your purpose and reason for existing? This exercise is one possible way of heeding Kierkegaard's advice to define life backward and then live it forward. You can write it purely as an exercise for yourself, or you can include it in your homegoing files or important documents, such as your will and funeral instructions.

GETTING STARTED

Following is one possible outline for how to structure your eulogy. It need not be followed in this exact order, and more than one paragraph may be needed for certain sections. There is no set length for a eulogy. Some suggest making it something that can be read in five to ten minutes, while others suggest a speech as long as twenty minutes. A general rule is 750 to 1,500 words in length.

Tip: Don't focus on the writing but the content. Others can word-smith it later if it is used as your obituary.

Paragraph 1: Introduction. Include your enduring reason for existing (a life purpose statement that encapsulates who you are).

Paragraph 2: Family and friends. Don't merely list closest relatives (e.g., spouse, children, parents) or best friends (if appropriate or desired) but also mention what these people meant to you and how you viewed and treasured these relationships. You can even paint a (brief) picture of what home life was like—the things you and your family enjoyed doing together.

Paragraph 3: Church and faith. Describe your faith journey, the community (or communities) where you fellowship, and any ministry involvement you hope to be remembered for. What spiritual gifts did God give you, and how did you invest them? What is your spiritual legacy?

Paragraph 4: Hobbies and interests. What did you do for fun? What subjects most captivated you? Did you have any secret (or little-known) skills or achievements?

Paragraph 5: Work/career. Summarize your vocational trajectory, both to date and anticipated (this will be an aspirational statement of some kind). You might start with schooling if that is important to you. Then emphasize activities and achievements of greatest import to you. How do you hope colleagues remember you? You can speak to volunteer work and work around the home as well if they aren't listed under your hobbies and interests.

Paragraph 6: Closing statement. Issue a final message that summarizes the legacy you hope to leave, along with any life mottos or Bible verses that sum up your life.

Acknowledgments

We would like to thank multiple individuals whose contributions played an important role in this book coming to fruition: Russ Crosson (of Ron Blue Trust), for his valuable input and contributions of content (especially for some of the tools) from the outset.

Michael Stewart, for his review of the first draft of the manuscript, plus his good counsel and encouragement throughout the publication process.

Matthew and Katie Robinson, for their valuable editorial assistance and suggestions for the manuscript.

William Kruidenier, for his helpful assistance with the purpose and stewardship chapters.

The many individuals who graciously shared their stories and thoughts on life transitions and recalibration in interviews of varying formats; their contributions brought concepts to life and reinforced the value of recalibration.

INDEX OF TOOLS

*Online only
**Expanded version online at recalibrateyourlife.org

TIPS ON USING THE TOOLS

The tools in this book form a robust set of exercises and resources for recalibrating throughout your life on a regular basis. They are especially helpful before, during, and after times of change and transition.

We recommend that you invest in a nice journal or notebook to take notes in so you can refer to them later. Call it your *Recalibration Journal*.

Revisit and review completed tools as needed. Following is a checklist suggesting the frequency of review for each tool.

Frequency to Revisit/Review	Tool
One-time (but revisit or update as needed)	4, 10, 13, 15, 17, 18
Annually (but update as needed)	2, 6, 7, 8, 11, 14
Monthly	5
Anytime	1, 3, 9, 12, 16

FIND A RECALIBRATION PARTNER

We urge you to find one other person who will commit to reading this book and using its tools with you. It's not necessary to use the same tools at the same time, but this person should be someone you can share your experiences with, discuss results, and keep one another accountable for follow-through with action items. This person may be your spouse or another family member, your best friend (or a close friend who is in the same stage of life as you), an existing mentor or coach, or someone you enjoy fellowship with (e.g., through church or a discipleship group or Bible study group). Ideally, this person will share at least one aspect of your current life stage with you.

Seven Keys to Living and Finishing Well

We should daily seek to live in the light of our true identity in Christ and in such a way that we will finish well whenever our time on this planet is up. The following seven keys to finishing well are important areas for seeking to grow continually.[1] Note that each key builds on the previous one, so if you are weak in an earlier one, focus on that one before working on the next one.

Being: Loving God Completely

Key 1. Intimacy with Christ. The Christian life entails the intentional pursuit to know Christ and put him first in our lives. To follow him we have to take time to get to know him, focusing more on this relationship than on sin management.

Key 2. Fidelity in the spiritual disciplines. As an athlete trains to compete and finish well, Christians need to train spiritually. Practices such as Bible study and reading and prayer (among many others) foster our intimacy with Christ. (Note: other disciplines include fasting, meditation, solitude and silence, chastity, secrecy, confession, submission to authority, stewardship, simplicity, fellowship, mentoring/guidance, celebration, sacrifice, and witness.)

---

[1]This list of keys first appeared in the first edition of Ken Boa, *Conformed to His Image.* They are described in more detail in Kenneth Boa, *Conformed to His Image: Biblical, Practical Approaches to Spiritual Formation*, rev. ed. (Grand Rapids, MI: Zondervan, 2020), 478-84. (The book is available at https://kenboa.org/product/conformed-to-his-image-revised -edition.)

Knowing: Loving Self Correctly

Key 3. A biblical perspective on the circumstances of life. God desires to use the trials and difficulties in our lives to drive us to greater reliance on and trust in him. We must view our ever-changing circumstances in light of his unchanging character rather than the other way around.

Key 4. A spirit of teachability, responsiveness, humility, and obedience. Those who finish well maintain an ongoing posture of learning throughout their lives. This posture requires humility and ongoing obedience to that which God teaches and reveals to us.

Key 5. A clear sense of personal purpose and calling. Your unique purpose or calling is your unchanging reason for being that holds true regardless of your circumstances in life (see tool 11). Transcending our occupations and enduring beyond retirement, your calling is the individual-level manifestation of God's universal purpose for believers: to know Christ and make him known (or edification and evangelism).

Doing: Loving Others Compassionately

Key 6. Healthy relationships with resourceful people. People who finish well do not do so without the support, encouragement, equipping, and exhortation of others. We need relationships that entail spiritual mentoring or guidance and accountability. These relationships help spur us on in all the other keys to finishing well.

Key 7. Ongoing ministry investment in the lives of others. We never reach a point where it's okay to withdraw or retire from ministry; there is no age limit on the Great Commission (or any of God's other commands about loving and serving other people). Those who finish well are marked by ongoing outreach and sacrificial ministry to the very end of their lives.

Scripture Guide for Transitions

Following are some verses of encouragement, guidance, and comfort that may be especially helpful during times of change and transition, loss, or adversity. These verses also offer anchoring truths and steady instruction to help you stay the course—living today in such a way that you will finish your life well, however much time you have left on this earth.

Leaning on the Eternal and Unchanging God
Psalm 46:6; 90:2; 102:11-12, 25-27; 103:17; 145:13
Isaiah 40:6-8
Daniel 7:14
Malachi 3:6
Matthew 24:35
Hebrews 13:8

Resting in Our Future Hope
Job 19:25-27
Psalm 37:28, 34; 39:4-7; 90:12, 17
Proverbs 23:18
John 10:27-29
Romans 8:18-25
2 Corinthians 4:14; 5:1-5
Ephesians 1:13-14
Philippians 3:20-21
Hebrews 6:13-20; 11:13, 16

1 Peter 1:3-5
1 John 2:17; 3:2-3

INVESTING IN THE ETERNAL OVER THE TEMPORAL
Proverbs 11:4; 11:28
Matthew 6:19-21, 33
1 Timothy 6:7
James 4:13-17
1 John 2:15-16

EMBRACING BIBLICAL STEWARDSHIP
Deuteronomy 8:11-14, 17-18
Proverbs 25:16
Ecclesiastes 7:11-12
Matthew 6:1, 24
Mark 12:43-44
Luke 12:15-21
1 Corinthians 4:7; 16:2
2 Corinthians 9:6-7
Colossians 3:23-24
1 Timothy 6:9, 17-19

FINDING COMFORT IN SUFFERING, TRIALS, AND LOSS
Deuteronomy 33:27
Psalm 23:4, 6; 46:1-5; 68:19; 119:50
Isaiah 43:2
Lamentations 3:19-24
Romans 5:3-5; 8:18
2 Corinthians 1:3-5; 4:16-18
Philippians 4:12-13
1 Peter 4:12-13; 5:10

FINISHING WELL

Psalm 71:17-18; 92:12-15

Mark 13:13

1 Corinthians 9:24-27

Galatians 6:9

1 Timothy 6:12-15

2 Timothy 2:11-13; 4:7-8

Hebrews 3:14; 6:11-12; 12:1-3

Revelation 13:10

Notes

Introduction: The Road Goes Ever On and On

[1] Appears in versions of the song in *The Fellowship of the Ring* and *The Return of the King*.

[2] J. R. R. Tolkien, *The Fellowship of the Ring: Being the First Part of the Lord of the Rings* (New York: Houghton Mifflin, 1954), 72.

[3] For more on this topic see Kenneth Boa with Jenny Abel, *Shaped by Suffering* (Downers Grove, IL: InterVarsity Press, 2020).

[4] Kenneth Boa, *Life in the Presence of God* (Downers Grove, IL: InterVarsity Press, 2017) and the companion Kenneth Boa and Jenny Abel, *A Guide to Practicing God's Presence* (Atlanta: Trinity House, 2018) deal with this theme.

[5] For further edification see "Seven Keys to Living and Finishing Well."

1. Leaving a Godly Legacy

[1] A. W. Tozer, *The Knowledge of the Holy* (New York: HarperCollins, 1961), 46.

[2] Similar passages also include Psalm 48:12-14 and Psalm 102:18, 25-28.

[3] This list is adapted from a longer list in Kenneth Boa, *Conformed to His Image: Biblical, Practical Approaches to Spiritual Formation*, rev. ed. (Grand Rapids, MI: Zondervan, 2020), 259-61.

2. Numbering Your Days

[1] The first part of the quote is found in William Brigham, *Historical Dictionary of Woody Allen* (Lanham, MD: Rowman and Littlefield, 2019), xiii. The second part of the quote is often attached to the first part but originates from a different place—"Woody Allen," *The Paris Review* 136 (Fall 1995), https://theparisreview.org/authors/5879/woody -allen.

[2] Jonathan Rauch, "The Real Roots of Midlife Crisis," *Atlantic*, December 2014, www .theatlantic.com/magazine/archive/2014/12/the-real-roots-of-midlife-crisis /382235.

[3] Rauch, "Real Roots of Midlife Crisis."

[4] The fear of God considers both his imminence (closeness to and love for us) and his transcendence (otherness from us). Ultimately, it results in an undying aim to please him above everyone and everything else.

[5] C. S. Lewis, *The Problem of Pain* (Nashville: Broadman & Holman, 1996), 83. The full quote is, "God whispers to us in our pleasures, speaks in our conscience, but shouts in our pains: it is His megaphone to rouse a deaf world."

[6] C. S. Lewis, *Letters to Malcolm: Chiefly on Prayer* (New York: Harvest, Harcourt Brace Jovanovich, 1964), 91.

3. Treasuring God and People

[1] *City Slickers*, directed by Ron Underwood (Culver City, CA: Columbia Pictures, 1991).

[2] Kenneth Boa, *Conformed to His Image: Biblical, Practical Approaches to Spiritual Formation*, rev. ed. (Grand Rapids, MI: Zondervan Academic, 2020), 12.

[3] Boa, *Conformed to His Image*, 95.

[4] Francis Schaeffer, *No Little People* (Downers Grove, IL: InterVarsity Press, 1974).

[5] Pamela Rosewell, *The Five Silent Years of Corrie ten Boom* (Grand Rapids, MI: Zondervan, 1986), 156, 157, 160, 162. Rosewell later married and became Pamela Rosewell Moore.

[6] Rosewell, *Five Silent Years*, 163.

4. Moving from Career to Calling

[1] Scott Harrison, "Meet the Founder," *Charity: Water*, accessed September 4, 2021, www .charitywater.org/about/scott-harrison-story. Thanks to Jordan Raynor and his book *Called to Create* for calling certain aspects of Harrison's life change and work to our attention.

[2] Harrison, "Meet the Founder."

[3] "Thirst," *Charity: Water*, accessed September 4, 2021, www.charitywater.org/thirst.

[4] Scott Harrison, quoted in Rachael Chong, "How the Founder of Charity: Water Went from Packing Clubs to Building Wells," *Fast Company*, December 10, 2012, www.fast company.com/2681043/how-the-founder-of-charitywater-went-from-packing-clubs -to-building-wells.

[5] Chong, "How the Founder of Charity."

[6] Jordan Raynor, *Called to Create: A Biblical Invitation to Create, Innovate, and Risk* (Grand Rapids, MI: Baker Books, 2017), 91-93.

[7] This language is borrowed from Gordon MacDonald, who discusses this discrepancy in-depth in *Ordering Your Private World* (Nashville: Thomas Nelson, 2003).

[8] Much of the content in this section is adapted from Kenneth Boa, *Conformed to His Image: Biblical, Practical Approaches to Spiritual Formation*, rev. ed. (Grand Rapids, MI: Zondervan, 2020), 245-47.

[9] This is discussed at length in Kenneth Boa, *Life in the Presence of God* (Downers Grove, IL: InterVarsity Press, 2017).

[10] Dorothy Sayers, *Letters to a Diminished Church: Passionate Arguments for the Relevance of Christian Doctrine* (Nashville: Thomas Nelson, 2004), 130-31.

[11] Skye Jethani, "Calling All Christians by Skye Jethani," *(re)integrate*, October 11, 2019, www.patheos.com/blogs/reintegrate/2019/10/11/calling-all-christians-by-skye -jethani.

[12] For more on this topic, we recommend Al Hsu, "Is All Work a High Calling?," *High Calling*, December 19, 2013, www.patheos.com/blogs/thehighcalling/2013/12/is-all -work-a-high-calling.

[13] Martin Luther King Jr., "'The Three Dimensions of a Complete Life,' Sermon Delivered at the Unitarian Church of Germantown," December 11, 1960, Stanford University's Martin Luther King, Jr. Research and Education Institute, https://kinginstitute .stanford.edu/king-papers/documents/three-dimensions-complete-life-sermon -delivered-unitarian-church-germantown.

[14] Finances will carry less weight for some than others.

[15] William Warren, quoted in Jordan Raynor, *Called to Create: A Biblical Invitation to Create, Innovate, and Risk* (Grand Rapids, MI: Baker Books, 2017), 54.

[16] Raynor, *Called to Create*, 54.

[17] I (Ken) was inspired to create the process described in this tool by PMI Shares's "SIMA" (System for Identifying Motivated Abilities), developed by Art Miller Jr. and first published in 1961. The first three steps bear similarities to the SIMA, but the fourth step is my own, and I have used it often to counsel people who are trying to determine how to spend their retirement years as well as people seeking greater fulfillment and enjoyment in their jobs/careers (by merging their occupations and their God-given giftings/callings). SIMA coaches offer in-depth analysis and private interviews/consulting to those who go through the SIMA process. You can find a SIMA Certified Coach at simainternational.com.

[18] Russ Crosson, *Your Life . . . Well Spent: The Eternal Rewards of Investing Yourself and Your Money in Your Family* (Eugene, OR: Harvest House, 2012), 82.

[19] Crosson, *Your Life*, 95.

[20] This material is adapted from tips by Crosson, *Your Life*, 94-95.

[21] Jeff Schmidt's book *Disciplined Minds: A Critical Look at Salaried Professionals and the Soul-Battering System That Shapes Their Lives* (Lanham, MD: Rowman & Littlefield, 2001) offers great insight into how professional work life today is designed to diminish individuality and force conformity to a strict ideological discipline (status quo). The result is that office jobs today tend to work against principles (like freedom and independent thinking) that enable us to work in a way that is consistent with Scripture. That being said, we should never consider ourselves merely as victims of a system or employer. God is still in control, and as his representatives in the world we still have the agency and true spiritual freedom that he brings, no matter how oppressive a work situation may be.

5. DEVELOPING A BETTER VISION OF RETIREMENT

1 Phil Burgess, *Reboot! What to Do When Your Career Is Over But Your Life Isn't* (Victoria, BC: Friesen Press, 2011), 29.

2 Burgess, *Reboot!*, 29-32.

3 Burgess, *Reboot!*, 32.

4 Burgess, *Reboot!*, 33.

5 Stephen M. Pollan and Mark Levine, "The Rise and Fall of Retirement," *Worth*, December–January 1995, 67.

6 Pollan and Levine, "Rise and Fall of Retirement," 70.

7 Pollan and Levine, "Rise and Fall of Retirement," 69.

8 Melissa Phipps, "The History of Pension Plans in the U.S.," *Balance*, accessed April 28, 2021, www.thebalance.com/the-history-of-the-pension-plan-2894374.

9 Kathleen Coxwell, "Average Retirement Income 2022: How Do You Compare?" New-Retirement, February 24, 2022, www.newretirement.com/retirement/average-retirement-income-2022-how-do-you-compare.

10 Mira Rakicevic, "30 Revealing Retirement Statistics and Facts for 2022," MedAlertHelp, December 20, 2020, https://medalerthelp.org/blog/retirement-statistics.

11 Rakicevic, "30 Revealing Retirement Statistics."

12 Pollan and Levine, "Rise and Fall of Retirement," 70.

13 Schulze's ideas are encapsulated in his book *Excellence Wins: A No-Nonsense Guide to Becoming the Best in a World of Compromise* (Grand Rapids, MI: Zondervan, 2019).

14 Russ Crosson, personal email to the authors, October 13, 2020. Crosson notes that this definition is based on that in the Merriam-Webster Dictionary.

15 Arthur C. Brooks, "Your Professional Decline Is Coming (Much) Sooner Than You Think," *Atlantic*, July 2019, www.theatlantic.com/magazine/archive/2019/07/work-peak-professional-decline/590650.

16 Daniel J. Levitin, *Successful Aging: A Neuroscientist Explores the Power and Potential of Our Lives* (New York: Dutton, 2020), xxi-xxii.

17 Levitin, *Successful Aging*, 138.

18 Levitin, *Successful Aging*, xiv.

19 Levitin, *Successful Aging*, xxiii.

20 Levitin, *Successful Aging*, xxii.

21 Technically, Jethro could have been younger than Moses; however, the point still stands since Jethro was in a position of respect as Moses' father-in-law.

22 Burgess speaks to this growing population in his book *Reboot!*, which we highly recommend to those who may have retired but are considering going back to work.

23 This material is borrowed and adapted, with permission, from Russ Crosson and colleagues at Ronald Blue Trust; the material has been presented in various places, including by Crosson at the Truth@Work Conference in September 2020.

6. Understanding God's Purposes

[1] Nancy Tillman, *You're Here for a Reason* (New York: Feiwel and Friends, 2015).

[2] Material in this section draws from various sources, including Kenneth Boa, *Conformed to His Image: Biblical, Practical Approaches to Spiritual Formation*, rev. ed. (Grand Rapids, MI: Zondervan, 2020), 488-93.

[3] God seeking his own glory is not narcissistic, as it would be for us. Unlike humans he *deserves* the highest adulation because he is the wellspring of all truth, goodness, and beauty.

[4] This question of why a God of love would create people who will never turn to him and will instead spend eternity in a place of punishment and pain (Proverbs 16:4) is hard for us to swallow. Yes, he is also a God of justice and cannot let evil go unpunished. In some mysterious, perfect combination of his love and justice, he gives his image-bearers free will (another hard-to-understand concept in a world under the control of a sovereign God) to choose him or not—to turn from their sin and trust him or to remain dead in sin and reject his free gift of eternal life.

[5] We wrote extensively about how God uses pain and suffering to shape us and conform us to his Son's image in our book *Shaped by Suffering* (Downers Grove, IL: InterVarsity Press, 2020); we recommend it to those going through a difficult time or who want to prepare well for future suffering.

[6] Boa, *Conformed to His Image*, 233.

[7] Boa, *Conformed to His Image*, 492.

7. Discovering Your Unique Purpose

[1] Boa, *Conformed to His Image*, 492.

[2] Boa, *Conformed to His Image*, 492.

[3] To further explore Jesus' unique purpose—and gain insight into what it means to discover and fulfill our own unique purpose in life—we recommend these verses in the Gospel of John: 4:34; 5:19, 30; 6:38; 7:16, 28-29; 8:26-29, 42; 10:37-38; 12:49; 14:10, 31; 15:10; 16:13; 17:4.

[4] Much of the material in this tool has been taken from "A Biblical View of Purpose, Part 2: Discerning God's Calling," *Ken Boa* (blog), November 14, 2017, https://kenboa .org/living-out-your-faith/a-biblical-view-of-purpose-part-2.

8. Stewarding All That God Gives

[1] John Newton, quoted in Jonathan Aitken, *John Newton: From Disgrace to Amazing Grace* (Wheaton, IL: Crossway, 2007), 24.

[2] Aitken, *John Newton*, 353.

[3] Aitken, *John Newton*, 354.

[4] Aitken, *John Newton*, 355.

[5] Aitken, *John Newton*, 24.

9. Stewarding Time

[1] The word used for "time" in Ephesians 5:16 is *kairos* or opportunity time (see chap. 1), as opposed to calendar time, *chronos*. The point is still salient, however, as we are to steward both kinds of time.

10. Stewarding Talent

[1] Courtney Ahlstrom Christy, "Julia Woodman," *Metalsmith* 39, no. 3 (2021): 20, https:// juliawoodman.com/wp-content/uploads/2020/10/Metalsmith-Vol-39-No-3 _Woodman.pdf.

[2] Christy, "Julia Woodman," 20.

[3] Christy, "Julia Woodman," 20.

[4] Julia Woodman, quoted in Christy, "Julia Woodman," 20.

[5] Christy, "Julia Woodman," 21.

[6] Woodman, quoted in Christy, "Julia Woodman," 21.

11. Stewarding Treasure

[1] *Wild Mountain Thyme*, directed by John Patrick Shanley (Los Angeles: Amasia Entertainment, 2020).

[2] First Timothy 6:17-19 discusses faithfulness in prosperity, but the principle extends to all of us (rich, poor, and everyone in between).

[3] These principles are adapted from teachings and writings of Ken Boa and from his co-authored book, Kenneth Boa and Russ Crosson, *Leverage: Using Temporal Wealth for Eternal Gain* (Atlanta: Trinity House, 2022). We highly recommend this book as a complement to this chapter.

[4] This famous phrase comes from C. S. Lewis, *The Last Battle*, Chronicles of Narnia (New York: HarperCollins, 2007, orig. 1956), 203, 207.

[5] A significant portion of this material is borrowed and adapted from Ron E. Dunn, *Unfinished Business: Putting Your Affairs in Order with Meaning and Purpose* (Atlanta: Ron Dunn, 2009), with permission. We recommend purchasing the book if you find this tool particularly useful. (It is available on Amazon.com.)

[6] Dunn, *Unfinished Business*, 17.

[7] Use tool 16 for a deep dive into organizing and gaining perspective on the financial aspects of your life.

[8] We greatly appreciate Russ Crosson's input on this tool, including content that is original to Ronald Blue Trust (borrowed and adapted with permission).

12. STEWARDING TRUTH

[1] Richard Dawkins, a British biologist and author of *The God Delusion*, is one of the best-known atheists of the twenty-first century (to date).

[2] Antony Flew, "Professor Antony Flew Reviews *The God Delusion*," *BeThinking* (blog), 2008, accessed May 14, 2022, www.bethinking.org/atheism/professor-antony-flew -reviews-the-god-delusion. See also Gary R. Habermas, "Farewell to an Old Friend: Remembering Antony Flew," *Philosophia Christi*, vol. 12, no. 1 (2010): 217.

[3] John Robinson, *Works of John Robinson* (London: John Snow, 1851), xliv, emphasis added.

[4] Robinson, *Works of John Robinson*, xliv.

[5] These points are taken from Kenneth Boa, *Conformed to His Image: Biblical, Practical Approaches to Spiritual Formation*, rev. ed. (Grand Rapids, MI: Zondervan, 2020), 422.

13. STEWARDING RELATIONSHIPS

[1] By tearing down the dividing lines between believers, Paul was not saying that there was no such thing as a biological male as distinct from a biological female, just as he was not denying the existence of other distinctions (in ethnicity, workplaces, and society). His point was that our unity in Christ takes precedence over those divisions. There is a level playing field in terms of our value and identity in Christ, with no class of Christian more important or more spiritual than another.

[2] This account is a true story, with names changed for the sake of anonymity. So far Henri hasn't placed his faith in Christ, but he has now heard the gospel message more than once and has had many discussions with Patrick thanks to the various interactions over years.

[3] Ron E. Dunn, *Unfinished Business: Putting Your Affairs in Order with Meaning and Purpose* (Atlanta: Ron Dunn, 2009), 197.

[4] Borrowed from Dunn, *Unfinished Business*, 197-99, used with permission

CONCLUSION: LIVING SO THAT THE BEST IS YET TO COME

[1] "God Is in the Details," John 10:10 Project, accessed October 9, 2021, https:// thejohn1010project.com/god-is-in-the-details.html.

[2] "God Is in the Details."

[3] John Donne, "Meditation 17," *The Complete Poetry and Selected Prose of John Donne*, ed. Charles M. Coffin (New York: Random House, 1952), 440. Spellings and capitalization have been updated to modern English.

[4] Jonathan Edwards, *Sermons and Discourses*, ed. Wilson H. Kimnach, vol. 10, *1720–1723*, Works of Jonathan Edwards, accessed November 13, 2021, http://edwards.yale.edu /archive.

[5] Pamela Rosewell, *The Five Silent Years of Corrie ten Boom* (Grand Rapids, MI: Zondervan, 1986), 183.

[6] Rosewell, *Five Silent Years*, 183-84.

[7] Rosewell, *Five Silent Years*, 186.

ABOUT THE AUTHORS

Kenneth Boa is engaged in a ministry of relational evangelism and discipleship teaching, writing, and speaking. He holds a BS from Case Institute of Technology, a ThM from Dallas Theological Seminary, a PhD from New York University, and a DPhil from the University of Oxford. Ken is engaged in a wide variety of ministry activities. He is the founder and president of Reflections Ministries, Omnibus Media Ministries, and Trinity House Publishers. On a local level he teaches multiple studies a week and leads small discipleship groups monthly. He is also engaged in one-on-one discipleship, mentoring, and spiritual direction. On a national and international level Ken speaks and teaches throughout the United States and in various countries. He lives in Atlanta with his wife of more than fifty years, Karen.

Jenny Abel is an editor and writer for Omnibus Media Ministries, founded by Ken Boa in 2018. Having sat under Boa's teaching since she was a teenager, she began working for him and his Reflections Ministries in 2013 and serves as editor of the monthly *Reflections* teaching letter. She cowrote *Shaped by Suffering* and *A Guide to Practicing God's Presence* with Ken Boa and edited *Life in the Presence of God*. Owner of Jenny M. Abel Editorial Services, she holds a BS in mathematics with a concentration in Latin American studies from Furman University, is a graduate of the Focus on the Family Leadership Institute, and resides in Charlottesville, Virginia, with her husband, Ben, and their two children.

MINISTRIES

REFLECTIONS MINISTRIES

Kenneth Boa founded Reflections Ministries in 1995. Its mission is to encourage, teach, and equip people to know Christ, follow him, become progressively conformed to his image, and reproduce his life in others. The ministry accomplishes this mission through local studies, special outreach events and conferences, and numerous written, audio, visual, and video resources.

Website: http://reflections.org

OMNIBUS MEDIA MINISTRIES

Founded by Kenneth Boa in 2018, Omnibus Media Ministries expands on Reflections Ministries' mission with a focus on the digital arena. Omnibus Media seeks to multiply disciples who invest the Word of God into the lives of others. It fulfills this vision by generating transformative media across multiple platforms, ranging from apps and websites to audiobooks and curricula. See some of its current offerings at presence.app and thomascoleart.com.

Website: http://omnibusmedia.com

TRINITY HOUSE PUBLISHERS

Trinity House Publishers, founded in 1993 by Kenneth Boa, is dedicated to the creation of tools that will help people manifest eternal values in a temporal arena by drawing them to intimacy with God and by encouraging a better understanding of the culture in which they live. Its publications include *Handbook to Prayer* (plus eight other titles in

a larger handbook series), *Jesus in His Own Words, A Guide to Practicing God's Presence,* and *Leverage: Using Temporal Wealth for Eternal Gain.*
Website: trinityhousepublishers.org

SOCIAL MEDIA

www.facebook.com/KennethBoa
www.instagram.com/ken.boa
twitter.com/kennethboa
youtube.com/c/ReflectionsMinistries

OTHER BOOKS
BY KEN BOA

AVAILABLE FROM INTERVARSITY PRESS

Faith Has Its Reasons

Life in the Presence of God

Passionate Living: Praises and Promises

Passionate Living: Wisdom and Truth

Rewriting Your Broken Story

Shaped by Suffering

ALSO BY KEN BOA

20 Compelling Evidences That God Exists

Augustine to Freud

Conformed to His Image

God, I Don't Understand

A Guide to Practicing God's Presence

Handbook to Leadership

Handbook to Prayer

Handbook to Renewal

Handbook to Scripture

I'm Glad You Asked

A Journal of Sacred Readings

Leadership in the Image of God

Talk Thru the Bible